The Couple

The Couple: A pluridisciplinary story asks two questions and endeavours to answer them: What is the couple? And what story are we talking about?

Éric Smadja presents his view of "the couple" as a composite, sexual-bodily, socio-cultural and psychic living reality in diverse and variable interrelationships, unfolding within a complex temporality. Ambivalently invested in by each partner, the couple is structurally and dynamically as conflictual as it is critical.

Smadja sees the couple as situated at the intersection of several histories: socio-cultural; epistemological (the construction of this object of knowledge and of psychoanalytic treatment); "natural" (that of the cycle of conjugal life marked out by critical and mutative stages) and therapeutic (that of the suffering couple that will consult a specialist and undergo psychoanalytic therapy). *The Couple: A pluridisciplinary story* follows the narrative division of these histories following a pluri- and interdisciplinary investigation combining historical, anthropological, sociological and psychoanalytic approaches. It enables the reader to structure the outline of a general, but irreducibly heterogeneous, picture of the couple, and by so doing, Smadja is able to develop new interdisciplinary concepts, in particular those of *couple work* and *conjugal culture*. In the final part of the book, he presents a full case study and introduces new technical aspects of this psychoanalytic work.

This unique approach to the study of the couple as a unit will appeal to psychoanalysts, especially those working with couples, psychologists, psychotherapists, psychiatrists, medical doctors, students and academics of psychoanalytic studies, anthropology and sociology.

Éric Smadja is a psychiatrist, a psychoanalyst, a member of the Société Psychanalytique de Paris and of the International Psychoanalytic Association (IPA), a couples psychoanalyst, and also an anthropologist and associate member of the American Anthropological Association. In 2007, he was awarded the IPA's Prize for "Exceptional Contribution Made to Psychoanalytic Research." He is the author of several books, many of which have been translated into English.

The Couple

A pluridisciplinary story

Éric Smadja

LONDON AND NEW YORK

First published in French 2011
By Presses Universitaires de France

First published in English 2016
by Routledge
2 Park Square, Milton Park, Abingdon, Oxon OX14 4RN

and by Routledge
711 Third Avenue, New York, NY 10017

Routledge is an imprint of the Taylor & Francis Group, an informa business

© Presses Universitaires de France, *Le Couple et Son Histoire*

The right of Éric Smadja to be identified as author of this work has been
asserted by him in accordance with sections 77 and 78 of the Copyright,
Designs and Patents Act 1988.

All rights reserved. No part of this book may be reprinted or reproduced
or utilised in any form or by any electronic, mechanical, or other means,
now known or hereafter invented, including photocopying and recording,
or in any information storage or retrieval system, without permission in
writing from the publishers.

Trademark notice: Product or corporate names may be trademarks
or registered trademarks, and are used only for identification and
explanation without intent to infringe.

British Library Cataloguing in Publication Data
A catalogue record for this book is available from the British Library

Library of Congress Cataloging in Publication Data
Names: Smadja, Éric.
Title: The couple : a pluridisciplinary story / Éric Smadja.
Other titles: Couple et son histoire. English
Description: 1 Edition. | New York : Routledge, 2016. | First published in
    France 2011. | Includes bibliographical references.
Identifiers: LCCN 2015046999| ISBN 9781138645721 (hardback) |
    ISBN 9781138645745 (pbk.) | ISBN 9781315627977 (ebook)
Subjects: LCSH: Couples. | Couples—Psychology. | Man-woman
    relationships—Social aspects.
Classification: LCC HQ801 .S626513 2016 | DDC 306.7—dc23
LC record available at http://lccn.loc.gov/2015046999

ISBN: 978-1-138-64572-1 (hbk)
ISBN: 978-1-138-64574-5 (pbk)
ISBN: 978-1-315-62797-7 (ebk)

Typeset in Times New Roman
by Swales & Willis Ltd, Exeter, Devon, UK

Contents

By way of introduction   viii

1   The couple's historical and socio-cultural envelope   1

Linguistic considerations regarding marriage and couples 1
General anthropological facts 3
A historical look at marriage and the couple in the
    Western world 4
Sociological facts of Western contemporary society 8

2   Some historical points of reference, or the construction
of an object of knowledge and of psychoanalytic treatment   11

Starting with Freud's writings 11
The notion of object-relation and its fates in the hands of
    different specialists 17
Melanie Klein 18
Post-Kleinians: Winnicott and Bion 20
Henry Dicks and Jürg Willi 25
Jean-Georges Lemaire 27
Group psychoanalysis and its impact in France 28
Some contemporary French conceptions 32

3   About some fundamental psychic components present
within the couple   39

The sexual, sexuality and the "erotic chain" 39
Narcissism and its different approaches 40
Instinctual and affective ambivalence 43
Some pregenital aspects 43
Concerning some major conflicts 44

vi Contents

Psychic bisexuality 46
Envy and jealousy 47
The Œdipus and sibling complexes 48
Fantasy life 48
Projections and identifications 49
The fusional and symbiotic aspects 50
Transference within the couple 51
Object-relations 51

4 Sketching a "natural" history of the couple 56

*The meeting, choice of partner and the couple's modalities of
   psychic structuring 56*
*The "honeymoon" and crisis in the couple: a psychoanalytical
   approach 62*
*Living together, or developing a conjugal culture
   and identity 67*
The couple and their desire for a child 79
From the couple to the family: the birth of a child 81
The childless couple, out of "free choice" or sterility 88
Growing old together 92

5 The concept of *couple work* 100

A necessary introduction to the concept of couple work *100*
Presentation of couple work *100*
*Reflections on the purposes, antagonisms and repercussions
   on the partners in* couple work *108*
The failures of couple work *109*
Normality and pathology in couples' lives together 110
Some functions of couple work *110*

6 The suffering couple, their request for consultation
   and the psychoanalytical work 113

Circumstances of the first consultation 113
The three preliminary interviews 114
Indications and contra-indications 118
Presentation and establishment of the framework 119
Technical aspects of the psychoanalytical work 119
Objectives and benefits 122
My work with Martine and Louis 123

Contents vii

By way of conclusion 132

The psychoanalyst's first reflections 135
Complementary reflections 136

Bibliography 139
Index 143

By way of introduction

The Couple: A pluridisciplinary story asks two questions and endeavors to answer them: What is the couple? And what story are we talking about?

Many writers, poets, novelists, philosophers, essayists, scientists, specialists in diverse fields, have explored this complex, composite reality that is the human heterosexual, as well as homosexual, couple. They have often confined their investigations and their discourse to one or a few aspects of the couple, associating it with: love, its nuances and inevitable vicissitudes; its components, processes and psychic productions; its sexual life, with its principles and its dysfunctions; the institution of marriage, its history, its rules, the ways it is portrayed and its culturally variable practices; the biological and social unit of reproduction; the unit of breeding and bringing up children (the parental couple); as well as the unit of economic and social cooperation based on a sexual distribution of common tasks; its history, with the changes and sociological characteristics of contemporary couples; legal aspects conferring status, rights and obligations to certain forms of conjugal – marital and non-marital, heterosexual and homosexual – union.

These many contributions to the subject have undeniably enriched our knowledge of the human couple. Nevertheless, they have done so compartmentally, leaving us, then, without the unified picture we are most in need of today, all the more so as we very frequently hear people talking, and without clearly identifiable reasons, about "couples in crisis," about the "crisis of contemporary couples," much as, moreover, we speak of "Western society in crisis," the two being inevitably inseparable.

Indeed, although considerably broadened and diversified, our present-day knowledge is thereby broken up correlatively. Yet the couple, as I view it in the present work, is a living human reality that is necessarily complex, because it is composite, integrating, like any other human reality, several orders of reality and situated at the intersection of several approaches.

Let me specify that I shall be dealing with heterosexual couples but that I shall, nonetheless, present some sociological information regarding homosexual couples in our times.

Thus, I shall envisage the socio-cultural, psychic and sexual-bodily dimensions unfolding within a complex temporality, whose interconnections, following modalities yet to be defined, will make this so enigmatic conjugal reality more comprehensible overall. To this end, I shall necessarily undertake a pluri- and interdisciplinary investigation, combining historical, anthropological, sociological and psychoanalytic approaches, which I hope will lead to much greater intelligibility because of its patently heuristic value. In addition, each one of these approaches will draw together the points of view of different experts.

In that regard, I am pursuing a research approach that I first used in my first book on laughter,[1] which has proved to be scientifically fruitful. I adopted it again in my preceding work,[2] which, taking the Œdipus complex as its point of departure, dealt with a historical and epistemological approach to the relationship between psychoanalysis and anthropology, and which has already inquired into the conditions conducive to engaging in pluri- and interdisciplinary research. On this point, I gladly take my place in an imaginary intellectual line of descent peopled by different thinkers, among them Sigmund Freud, Marcel Mauss, Géza Róheim, Georges Devereux and, more recently, Edgar Morin, especially. Remember that Mauss (1924) already defined all social facts as being "total"[3], because they integrate multiple, interdependent components – historical, economic, political, ideological, technological, ecological and those involving kinship, for example – whose discovery made those facts intelligible. Moreover, he advocated an exploration of the "total" person, with his or her historical, socio-cultural, bodily and psychic dimensions, the latter, however, involving a psychological, non-psychoanalytic investigation, with regard to which he expressed reticence based on serious lack of understanding. I share his viewpoint concerning the exploration of the "total person" using our contemporary scientific knowledge and methods, and underpinned by a solid epistemological reflection, procuring for us conditions conducive to pluri- and interdisciplinary research.

But the couple is also situated, as I said, at the intersection of several histories that I am proposing to discuss: socio-cultural; epistemological (the construction of this object of knowledge and of psychoanalytic treatment); "natural" (that of the cycle of conjugal life marked off by critical and mutative stages); and, finally, therapeutic (that of the suffering couple that will consult a specialist and undergo psychoanalytic therapy).

So, *The Couple: A pluridisciplinary story* will follow the narrative division of several histories chosen and dealt with following a pluri- and interdisciplinary approach that will enable us to compare specialized discourses and identify certain convergences, divergences and complementarities, contributing, then, to structuring the outline of a general, but irreducibly heterogeneous, picture of the couple.

The history, the social organization of every society, its diverse social relationships, the multiple symbolic systems that it elaborates and produces, the modalities of its self-preservation, of its production and reproduction envelop and structure this human reality that is the couple. That is why I have first of all chosen, in Chapter 1, to peel away its historical and socio-cultural envelope.

Then, in Chapter 2, I plan to go through certain stages of the genesis of the construction of this new epistemological object – an object of psychoanalytic knowledge and of treatment that the couple has become in our contemporary Western society characterized by prevalent individualism. It is, moreover, this

x By way of introduction

social individualism that has made possible the emergence of the Western couple, distinguishing itself from the institutional framework of marriage. Via the "antagonism" of individual and conjugal interests, we shall find again the primordial antagonism between the individual and society, which Emile Durkheim (1893) explored so well,[4] at the heart of the contemporary couple.

Chapter 3, which deals with the couple's fundamental psychic components, is exclusively psychoanalytical. It enables one to demonstrate the full complexity of the conscious, preconscious and unconscious psychic reality present through its "materials" and at work in the organization and functioning of every couple. In addition, it prepares one for the discovery and intelligibility of its "natural" history.

Chapter 4 recounts, therefore, this "natural" history through certain particularly significant periods chosen for their "mutative" and maturing critical characteristics. Here, I regularly compare several approaches – anthropological, sociological and psychoanalytic.

This is where my pluri- and interdisciplinary approach, which attempts consistently to connect the discourse of specialists with particular conceptions formulated about well-circumscribed aspects, becomes pertinent to today's realities in the clearest way. Readers will then grow aware of the radical heterogeneity of certain points of view reflecting such different and such conflictualized orders of reality organizing all human reality. They will thus attempt to unify them.

In Chapter 5, I present and develop a new concept of an interdisciplinary nature, that of *couple work*, a psychoanalytical and socio-anthropological concept, by which I endeavor to demonstrate the couple's pluri-dimensionality, modes of connecting its diverse levels, its organization and its functioning, but also its dysfunctioning. It is a matter of a "working" hypothesis, whose value as a mode of operation will have to be evaluated.

Finally, the last chapter retraces the course taken by suffering couples who finally decide to ask for help by consulting a specialist, a therapist for couples, particularly one trained in psychoanalysis. I shall describe its principal phases, from the circumstances of the first consultation to the objectives and benefits expected of psychoanalytic therapy with couples. I offer readers a clinical illustration through Martine and Louis, one of the many couples I have received.

By the time I reach the end of these many historical accounts, as well as of this pluri- and interdisciplinary exploration of the couple, I shall certainly have challenged a certain number of obvious facts that seem to me to have become "natural," while they resulted from historically, socio-culturally and psychically constructed processes.

Notes

1 Eric Smadja (2013), *Laughter*. London: College Publications. Translation of *Le Rire*. Paris: Presses universitaires de France, 1993, 1996, 2007, 2011.
2 Eric Smadja (2009), *Le complexe d'Œdipe, cristallisateur du débat psychoanalyse/anthropologie*. Paris: Presses universitaires de France.
3 Marcel Mauss (1924), "Essai sur le don," in *Sociologie et anthropologie*. Paris: Presses universitaires de France, 1950, pp. 145–279.
4 Emile Durkheim (1893), *Division of Labor in Society*. New York: Free Press, 1997.

Chapter 1

The couple's historical and socio-cultural envelope

Linguistic considerations regarding marriage and couples

On marriage

In the chapter entitled "The Indo-European Expression for 'Marriage'" of his book *Indo-European Language and Society*,[1] the linguist Emile Benveniste wrote that the Indo-European vocabulary surrounding kinship, for as long as it has been studied, has taught that in conjugality the situation of the man and that of the woman had nothing in common, just as the terms designating their respective kinship were completely different. *This is why there is not, strictly speaking, any Indo-European term for "marriage."*[2] In fact, the expressions found today would all be secondary creations, be it *mariage* (in French), *Ehe* (in German) or *brak* (in Russian), for example. In ancient languages, the facts seem to him to be more specific, and it would be of interest to tackle them in their diversity. Thus, the terms differ, especially, according to whether it is a matter of a man, for whom they would be *verbs*, or a woman, for whom they would be *nouns*.

According to Benveniste, to say that a man "takes a wife," Indo-European language uses the forms of the verbal root *wedh-* "to lead," especially "to lead a woman to the home." This particular meaning would be the result of close correspondences obtaining among most languages. Such was the expression in the most ancient state, and when certain languages renewed the notion of "to lead," the new verb also became the equivalent of "to marry (a woman)." This is what happened in Indo-Iranian, for example. In Latin, we find a new verb having the meaning of "to lead." It is *ducere*, which also acquires the meaning of "to marry" in *uxorem ducere*.

Those verbs referring to the role of the girl's father in the marriage, or for want of one, that of the brother, correspond to: "giving" the girl to her husband. "To give" is the verb consistently used for this solemn act; one finds it from one language to another, with at the very most some variations in the verb's prefix.

Benveniste argues that this consistency shows the persistence of ritual practices inherited from a common history and the same family structure, where the husband "led" the young woman whom her father had "given" him to his home.

2   The couple's historical and socio-cultural envelope

How about the woman's point of view? For her, there was no verb denoting the fact of marrying that would be the counterpart of the expressions mentioned. In Latin, for example, as an active verb *maritare* signifies "to pair up, to conjoin." So, the lack of her own verb indicates that the woman does not marry; she is married. She does not perform an act; her social status changes. However, that is precisely what the terms denote – the married woman's state. Here, it is exclusively a matter of *nouns* appearing on opposite branches of the Indo-European language tree, in Indo-Iranian and in Latin, that are used in the locution solemnly stating that the woman is taking on the "social status of wife." In Vedic, for example, *janitvana*, the term we would translate by "marriage," only applies to the woman and signifies a girl's accession to the state of legal wife. One might see in this a feature of "high Antiquity" linked with the structure of the great Indo-European family, for we find it in Roman society. The Latin term *matrimonium* is very significant in this regard. Taken literally, *matrimonium* signifies "legal status of *mater*." It therefore defines the social status to which the girl is acceding, that of *mater* (*familias*). That is what "marriage" signifies for her, not an act, but a destination; she is given and led away "in view of *matrimonium*," *in matrimonium*, just like the similar Indo-Iranian terms of *janitvana* – designating the state to which the bride is promised. The modern forms of *matrimonium* – *matrimonio* in the romance languages Spanish and Italian – have acquired the general meaning of "marriage." And this derivative *matrimonial* functions today in French as the adjective corresponding to *mariage*, so that, Benveniste observes, one might easily take *matrimonial* for the Latin derivative of *mariage*. However, *mariage*, the normal derivative of *marier* (Latin, *maritare*) has nothing in common with *matrimonium*. But the fact that the two have become associated with one another to the point of seeming related shows how far removed we are from ancient values. So it is that the noun forms that have led to the notion of "marriage" all first referred to the social status of the woman who became a wife. It was necessary for this specific feature to be expunged for the abstract concept of "marriage" to acquire substance and finally be able to designate the legal union of a man and a woman.

French definitions of "couple"

Now, what do we learn about the word *couple* from Emile Littré's *Dictionnaire de la langue française*?[3]

> It is a matter of a *bond* attaching together two or several *similar things* (a cord used to bind two hunting dogs together, for example).

> It is said, by extension, of *two things* of the *same kind, taken together*: a couple of eggs, of napkins.

> A husband and wife, a male lover and a female lover, or two people living together out of friendship or mutual interest.

Term of mechanics: name given to two equal, parallel forces acting in opposite directions, one of which is applied to one end of a lever, the other to the other.

When "couple" is used with the masculine article in French, it refers to *two people united together by love or by marriage*; the same is said of two animals united to copulate.

When used with the feminine article in French, "couple" refers to any two things of the same kind that do not necessarily go together at all, and are only united accidentally, while "pair" designates two things that go together because they have to be used that way, like socks, shoes. "Couple" in the feminine only denotes the number and pair, and adds to this the idea of a necessary association for a particular end.

Thus, through these multiple meanings and notions of *couple*, in the masculine and in the feminine – those of a bond attaching similar things, of equal and opposite forces, of two things of the same kind, of pair, of persons living together, united out of love or by marriage – Littré already affords us a glimpse of all the heterogeneity of this reality that we are going to explore.

General anthropological facts

Images of marriage, of married couples and of celibacy in traditional societies

In *Masculin/Feminin* (1996),[4] Françoise Héritier reminds us that kinship is the general matrix of social relationships, that society only exists divided into groups based on kinship and that it overcomes this original division through cooperation of which marriage, the primary institution, is one of the modalities opening into solidarity among these groups. She explains that a group that only counts on its own internal forces to reproduce biologically, that practices incest and only incest, would ultimately disappear, be it only through the rarefaction of its members.[5] This is why the law of exogamy, the foundation of any society, must be understood, according to her, as a law of exchange of women among groups, an exchange of life, because women give birth to children and give their power of fecundity to people other than their close relations.

Regarding the matter of procreative union, Héritier points out that one finds in all human societies, without exception – including those where no stable, permanent conjugal bond exists – a legitimate form that we conventionally call "marriage." It corresponds to extremely variable criteria. And it is this legitimate union that primarily constitutes the legitimacy of the children and *ipso facto* establishes their affiliation to a group.

But marriage is "serious business" involving adults, hence, the importance in this domain, as well, of rules of marriage enabling people to make choices that mitigate as much as possible the hazards and risks of ill-starred meetings. For, as Héritier explains, the punishment for mingling "incompatible blood" not accepted by the ancestors will be the sterility of the union or the early death of the children.[6]

4 The couple's historical and socio-cultural envelope

In the different human societies, marriage is also a state of economic cooperation, in which the two sexes use technical skills that their culture recognizes as theirs, dictated by social conventions. Thus, the sexual distribution of tasks is the point making the union of the man and the woman indispensable for the well-being of both and for the survival of society.

Nevertheless, besides this legitimate union several types of matrimonial union having a different status may be recognized, among them cohabitation.

In addition, most human societies are protected from primary celibacy – antisocial act *par excellence* and, at the same time, the very negation of the individual, who is only supposed to attain complete self-fulfillment in and through marriage. So-called primitive societies do not tolerate it, for either sex, in its Western form of a free individual choice constituting a life commitment. Moreover, there exists a difference of perception of celibacy as practiced by men and by women: men harm themselves, while women are dangerous for the collectivity. Generally conceived of as going against nature, as a crime against the ancestors, especially, primary celibacy may, however, be admitted or recommended in certain societies for economic reasons, for example, something observed in feudal society.

A historical look at marriage and the couple in the Western world

Let us engage in an overview of marriage in the Western world from its ancient origins up until our time with two historians, Jean-Claude Bologne (2005)[7] and André Burguière (1986).[8]

The legacy of the Romans and the Germanic peoples

Among both the Romans and the Germanic peoples, marriage first and foremost emerged from family laws and they knew two types of unions: on the one hand, an official marriage, decided upon by the family, on the other hand, a less stable union, *concubinat* among the Romans, *Friedelehe*, "lover marriage" among the Germanic peoples. It is to be noted that cohabitation also existed throughout the ancient Orient. Against that, the Church would attempt to put forward its conception of a single marriage.

The Christian conception of marriage

It was not until the end of the twelfth century that the canonic law for marriage would be drawn up, which was in fact a sacrament substantially constituted by the mutual consent of the spouses, whose ministers were the spouses themselves. The permission of the parents, even in the case of minor children, was not actually indispensable, no more than was the presence of witnesses or the intervention of a priest. Moreover, canon law specified numerous impediments to marriage. Finally, the sacrament of marriage was indissoluble. Only death could break the conjugal bond and thus free the surviving spouse to marry again. At the beginning of the sixteenth century, this conception of marriage was vigorously contested by the Protestant reformers, Luther and Calvin, whose positions would be condemned by the Council of Trent as early as 1547. They in fact considered marriage to be a divine institution, but not a sacrament. It was a contract based on mutual consent involving so great a commitment of spiritual and material interests as to need to be carefully thought over. In the case of minor children, this presupposes the obligatory consent of the parents expressing the authority of God without, nevertheless, imposing too many constraints upon them. Finally, Protestants theoretically accepted divorce, in the full sense of the term, but only in the case of proven adultery, or prolonged abandonment of the conjugal home. It was only in 1563 that the Council of Trent confronted the issue of matrimonial right and that very year adopted a body of texts including, notably, twelve very short canons reaffirming the sacramental, monogamous and indissoluble character of marriage, the primacy accorded to procreation, as well as the Church's exclusive competence in the matter of matrimonial causes. Moreover, a disciplinary decree targeted, in particular, clandestine marriages, that is those celebrated henceforth in the absence of the parish priest or of some other priest authorized by the parish priest. Finally, priestly celibacy was imposed and the state of virginity remained superior to that of marriage.

The Middle Ages, in feudal society

Feudal marriages were always a family affair, essentially concerning the fathers and secondarily the husband and wife. In fact, in the feudal system, starting in the Middle Ages, the court nobility particularly displayed overall suspicion in the face of love, which they tried to exclude from marriage in order to confine it within what was called "courtly love." The goal of marriage was to ensure the transmission of the fiefdom, without dividing up the land, to preserve the continuance of a mode of production. The nobility found it hard to comply with ecclesiastic legislation, engendering continual pressures and tensions between the two in the course of history. As a consequence, one often finds solemn marriage, alone in ensuring heirs, reserved for the oldest son, and therefore limited to one child per family. The younger children, if they did not make religious vows, were reduced to less noble or less durable forms of unions.

The Renaissance

This era was characterized by a general climate of sexual permissiveness, a state of mind favorable to the conjugal bond and an encouragement to individual determination. Although the marriage candidates were not alone in deciding and although negotiating such a marriage continued mainly to bring together two family groups having to work out between themselves a "transfer of woman and of goods," these young people did nevertheless enjoy a certain degree of autonomy of choice. In addition, we observe the first beginnings of a "paradoxical" privatization and

6 The couple's historical and socio-cultural envelope

autonomy gain among the couples because of a weakening of local community control combined with the reinforcing of the power of the family and centralized apparatuses, the Church among them.

Thus, the historian André Burguière considers that the conjugality advocated by the Church and by certain strata of civil society, and the increasingly asserted tendency to allow young people follow their hearts when it came to marrying and to respect the couple's autonomy took on new significance within this climate of tolerated sensuality and widespread Epicureanism. More precisely, they prepared the way for an inversion of the relationships between marriage and sexuality.[9] They constituted a first stage in the formation of the conjugal couple.

The problem of living together outside of marriage did not arise until after the Christianization of Europe when a single type of marriage was admitted. According to Bologne, it was really born with the Council of Trent, which relegated couples who lived together without having been married by a priest to the status of illegitimate cohabitation.

The Classical period

At this time, marriage began to be defined as a contract, a well-thought out act intended to ensure the good functioning of civil society and the preservation of fortunes in their initial state. This essentially static society had an aversion for everything that could set it back into motion. Love itself, that "devouring passion," which people ended up analyzing as an illness, was called upon to subject itself to reason. This search for balance, Bologne points out, was most particularly evident in the marriage contracts, where notaries assumed an increasingly important role over the course of these centuries, and in all classes of society.

Moreover, throughout Europe, State and Church exercised increasingly tight control over marriage and family. In France, especially, from that time on, no milieu escaped this twofold control, guarantor of parental authority and the social order.

The Enlightenment

If marriage and love were far from being incompatible during the seventeenth and eighteenth centuries, it was their natural order that was contested, Bologne explains. In fact, if it was not systematically forbidden to love one's wife or one's husband, it was unseemly to marry for love. Conjugal love was a serene feeling that was born after marriage and could not be its cause. Nevertheless, Burguière emphasizes that it would be absurd to claim that no one married for love, or that no couple was genuinely in love prior to the eighteenth century.[10]

I have already mentioned matrimonial alliances for love tolerated during the sixteenth century, in particular. In fact, an affective disposition of that kind neither constituted an ideal, nor was it necessary. Burguière explains that what should, therefore, be analyzed is the process by which love, long considered by religious morality and by popular wisdom as alien, and even contrary to marriage, became

The couple's historical and socio-cultural envelope   **7**

the keystone of a new matrimonial model.[11] According to him, such an evolution would rather derive from the interiorization of moral norms and models of conduct imposed by the Church, awakening in each individual a keener awareness of his or her responsibility and singularity that would then seek to be fulfilled in emotional fusion with another self. Yet, the "peripheral" or "popular" cultures continued, for their part, to refer to other models, notably that of a hierarchical society, more or less tempered by the ideological intervention of Church and State, which ensured a certain mediation between individual aspirations and family imperatives. The social constraints of the alliance, henceforth accepted by everyone, no longer seemed to be in contradiction with individual aspirations. But that only concerned certain social milieus.

Burguière expands upon his ideas about the changes affecting the diverse conditions and modalities operative in the formation of the couple and within the very climate of conjugal life during this period of European history. From among the multiple hypotheses and schemas of interpretation formulated by historians and sociologists, he has espoused the particularly persuasive ideas of the sociologist Norbert Elias, developed in his major two-volume work *Über den Prozess der Zivilization* (1939), subsequently published in English translation as *The History of Manners* and *State Formation and Civilization* and now available in a single volume entitled *The Civilizing Process: Sociogenetic and Psychogenetic Investigations.*[12]

Appealing to Elias's conception of the *civilizing process*, Burguière argues that it was during this long period of inculcation of an austere conjugal morality and surveillance of family life that the boundary line between the public and the private domains was more clearly drawn, carving out a sphere of intimacy within which the couple ceased to be a simple reproductive unit, in order to become a privileged pole of affection and solidarity. Paradoxically, it was also the religious redefinition of the bond of matrimony and the Church's effort to lock sexuality into the conjugal sphere that created the conditions for the emergence of marrying for love. Moreover, according to Burguière, in talking about marrying for love as the dominant matrimonial model, people confuse two distinct aspects that ended up merging, but after having run different courses: (1) the idea that young people themselves must be able to decide about the choice of their spouses; (2) that love determines their decision.

The nineteenth century

Love would demand to be present, in its romantic, passionate form right from the beginning of the nineteenth century. Confusing the sentiment with its manifestations (sexual freedom, freedom of choice), it would take as its models, according to Bologne, the lower classes and peasants who, free of the onerous system of dowry, could not, to the bourgeois mind, solely respond to noble sentiments. A new kind of life expressed new mentality, notably the possibility of having a genuine conjugal life, in the intimacy of personal living quarters, which afforded young couples the privacy impossible in traditional family homes (aristocratic

8 The couple's historical and socio-cultural envelope

town houses or country estates). The basic unit of society increasingly became the couple and not the extended family. This generalization of the conjugal family and the feelings of love it made obligatory constituted one of the major social mutations of the twentieth century. So, in France, marrying for love therefore developed slowly during the Third Republic and it would be in 1896 – to curb the crisis brought on by the very recent reestablishment of divorce – that a series of dispositions would be proposed tending to make the marital state easier and more financially accessible, above all for the poor, obliged to cohabitate in those days. Finally, living together was practiced more widely beginning in the twentieth century, essentially in the urban milieus and among the poorer and working classes.

The twentieth century

At the beginning of the twentieth century, love in marriage was more topical than ever. However, marrying for financial reasons did not suddenly disappear. Only the very high strata of society were still sensitive to the attraction of dowries, along with people living in the country. However, following the First World War and the economic crisis, marriage, like society, underwent a crisis. And literature, political and religious moralists, as well as new laws, would profoundly modify the image of the couple. Something new was observed: the will to go further than the free expression of love for which the nineteenth-century romantic fought. If love increasingly was becoming a determining factor in marriage, it was not enough to guarantee conjugal happiness and young people considered that it was not destined to last a lifetime. Civil marriage progressively became a part of the mores of society, and the Church abandoned most of its claims in order to limit them to moral obligations regarding divorce and remarriage.

Sociological facts of Western contemporary society

The new modes of forming couples

Since the end of the 1960s, the structure of the couple has been rapidly and profoundly turned upside down, according to the sociologist Jean-Claude Kaufmann (2007).[13] He has detected a transformation of the internal processes of the formation of couples, of which he identifies two models: marriage and the couple "little by little," monitored and gradual settling down.

In fact, he considers that today marriage is beginning to change its form and, above all, its place and function in the conjugal cycle. It used to be the basis of the couple; more and more, it tends to complete it. It used to establish a setting for socialization; more and more, it tends to institutionalize the setting for socialization previously set in place. The earlier type of marriage marked a sudden break from one's youth, in the family into which one was born, and entry into adult life. In comparison, the majority of young people are now gradually beginning to live as couples, little by little.[14]

Just as specialists (historians, sociologists and demographers, in particular) as a whole emphasize the *historical and mutative* transition from a traditional institutional definition of the couple through marriage to an internal and largely intersubjective definition of the contemporary couple that is no longer guaranteed, or so very little, by the institutions, contemporary couples have become unstable, fragile and, since the 1970s, a number of indicative statistics testify to this: the lowering of the marriage rate, the increase in the number of people living together, and in heterosexual and homosexual relationships, divorces and separations, but, above all, the decline in the life of couples living together and the rise in the number of persons living alone. However, the latter are for all that not without a sexual life or partners. They have chosen a less committed, therefore, looser, form of conjugal organization that is emblematic of contemporary couples. In addition, these scholars have spotted the central role of sexuality – in both forming and sustaining conjugal relationships – then becoming the "basic language of the relationship,"[15] the shortcomings of which today represent a factor threatening breakdown in relationships. And on that level, we find a historically new convergence of expectations and demands on the part of men and women, especially as concerns "sexual continuity," principally before the birth of children.

What about homosexual couples?

At one time or another, most homosexuals have the experience of stable relationships or relationships as a couple, half of which involve living together, in contrast to heterosexual couples, a higher percentage of which live together, according to Michel Bozon. Taking the form of demands, their present desire to marry and have a child represents, as Maurice Godelier (2004)[16] has noted, something new and unprecedented in history. In addition, sexuality seems to play an even more important role than among heterosexuals. Sociological studies show that among "gay" couples, the presence of other partners is integrated into the conjugal functioning, as a manifestation of individual autonomy. However, among lesbian couples, the requirement for fidelity would seem to be much more inflexible. One trait specific to the relationships of homosexual couples would be that they are much less dependent than other couples on social and material commitments to stabilize them: purchase of a place to live, acquisition of goods held in common, children, a common network of friends, shared leisure activities. They tend to split up more quickly than heterosexual couples. However, the course of the relationships of homosexual couples also presents similarities with that of heterosexual couples. Thus, after a nascent phase, marked by intense affective commitment, frequent sexual relations, less interest in outside sexual partners, lasting couples experience a dulling of emotions and an increased recourse to extra-conjugal partners.

A pluri- and interdisciplinary exploration of the homosexual conjugal world should be undertaken.

Notes

1 Emile Benveniste (1969), *Indo-European Language and Society*. Coral Gables, FL: University of Miami Press, 1973, Book 2, Chapter 4, p. 197.
2 My emphasis.
3 Emile Littré (2007), *Dictionnaire de la langue française*. Paris: Encyclopedia Universalis, 2007.
4 Françoise Héritier (1996), *Masculin/Feminin, La pensée de la différence*. Paris: Odile Jacob.
5 *Ibid.*, p. 232.
6 *Ibid.*, p. 122.
7 Jean-Claude Bologne (2005), *Histoire du mariage en Occident*. Paris: Hachette.
8 André Burguière (1986), "La formation du couple," in André Burguière, Christiane Klapisch-Zuber, Martin Segalen and Françoise Zonabend (eds), *Histoire de la famille*, Vol. 3, *Le choc des modernités*. Paris: Armand Colin. English translation: *History of the Family*. Cambridge, MA: Belknap, 1996.
9 *Ibid.*, p. 158.
10 *Ibid.*, p. 179.
11 *Ibid.*, p. 179.
12 Norbert Elias (1939), *Über den Prozess der Zivilization*. Basel: Haus zum Falken, 1939. English translation: *The Civilizing Process: Sociogenetic and Psychogenetic Investigations*. Oxford: Blackwell Publishers, 2000 (revised edition).
13 Jean-Claude Kaufmann (2007), *Sociologie du couple*. Paris: Presses universitaires de France.
14 *Ibid.*, pp. 50–1.
15 Michel Bozon (2009), *Sociologie de la sexualité*. Paris: Armand Colin.
16 Maurice Godelier (2004), *Métamorphoses of Kinship*. London: Verso, 2011. Translation of *Métamorphoses de la parenté*. Paris: Fayard, 2004.

Chapter 2

Some historical points of reference, or the construction of an object of knowledge and of psychoanalytic treatment

Starting with Freud's writings

In my opinion, Freud discovered and set in place the fundamental psychic components of human love lives, but this was not yet a matter of a psychoanalysis of couples understood as an entity, a group, a dyad, with its structure, its functioning, its interactional dynamic, its drive economy and its history. It seems to me that a certain number of his texts represent major stages in his understanding of human love life. I shall present them in order to draw out their essential contributions. However, I consider it pertinent to situate human love life within the more general framework of the Freudian conception of object and object-relation beforehand.

Some words of explanation about the Freudian conception of object and object-relation

Several specialists, among them Bernard Brusset,[1] have detected the existence of two-sidedness of the object present from the beginning in Freud's work and generating a fundamental contradiction. It is an element constitutive of the drive and of the assembling of drives, interchangeable, but indispensable: no drive without an object. In addition, the object is also external to the drive, belonging to the external world, perceived, represented. It is aimed at and invested by the drive in such a way as to be perceived by the subject as a cause of desire. In the theoretical model of the development leading to objectal love, the external object appears as a pole of investment, vector of libidinal development, from pre-genitality toward genitality, having, therefore, organizational value. The genital object-relation is, in fact, a dimension present in Freud from the beginning.

The meaning of the notion of object-relation, as it can be established from the stages of Freud's work that are significant in this regard, describes a process going from the drive – and, thereby, from the implicit reference to the deviant sexual act – to object love. Afterward, it takes into account the narcissistic components and ambivalence of any object-relation. In addition, Freud began with the drive–object-relation and was led to the Ego–object-relation, to the point of making the Ego the site of objects introjected and lost as external objects.

12   Some historical points of reference

Finally, Brusset considers that, in Freud, the place of the object-relation stands in relationship to two poles: the first, that of sexuality, remains constant, while the second would first be self-preservation, then narcissism and, finally, the death drive. This triple dualism lends sexuality its central place.

Three Essays on the Theory of Sexuality (1905)[2]

Freud envisaged certain characteristics of the sexual drive as involving a measure of ascendancy and as aspiring to master the psychically overestimated sexual object. He described the characteristic features of infantile sexuality, the diphasic development of human sexuality, the latent phase and the changes occurring at puberty: the assembling of partial drives under the primacy of the genital; the selfish sexual drive becoming altruistic, its goal being henceforth genital and at the service of reproduction; the converging of the two currents, tender and sensual, toward the same object and the same genital goal being accomplished; the choice of object also being made in two phases, the "discovery" of the object is in fact a rediscovery. A first type of choice is described: anaclitic (dependent), connected with the woman who cared for the child. Perversions are described as a disorder of sexual development deriving from a fixation on certain aspects of infantile sexuality. Finally, he observed a certain fetichization of love life.

Contributions to the psychology of love life (1910; 1912; 1918)

In the 1912 text, *On the Universal Tendency to Debasement in the Sphere of Love*,[3] Freud described a splitting in the love life of certain men who manifest an unconscious incestuous fixation leading them to hold sexuality at a distance from objects of love, because if they do not, they would awaken the incestuous fixation. "Where they love they do not desire and where they desire, they cannot love."[4] So they choose objects defensively in order to avoid incest. This is the first psychoanalytical reflection upon a type of choice of love object that is defensive in nature. These men therefore need to debase the sexual object psychically, while the incestuous object and its substitutes are over-evaluated.[5] This same text also contains reflections on the psychical impotence of civilized men, the characteristics of Western love life, where the union of the two currents would not be very frequent, according to Freud. The man's sexual frustrations are discussed:

> the man almost always feels his respect for the woman acting as a restriction on his sexual activity and only develops full sexual potency when he is with a debased sexual object; and this in its turn is partly caused by the entrance of perverse sexual components into his sexual aims, which he does not like to satisfy with a woman he respects . . . Anyone who is to be really free and happy in love must have surmounted his respect for women and have come to terms with the idea of incest with mother or sister.[6]

Some historical points of reference 13

However, in *The Taboo of Virginity* (1918a),[7] it is a matter of the woman's unconscious desire for castration, correlate of her envy of the man's penis, which can lead to pathological defensive manifestations like frigidity.

On Narcissism: An Introduction (1914)[8]

This very rich text discusses primary and secondary narcissisms, the contrast or dualism between the narcissistic libido and objectal libido, and its economic problem. The more absorbing the one is, the more the other is impoverished, which is a unilateral, non-interactional view of libidinal movements between the Ego and its object. The essay presents the two types of object-choice: anaclitic (dependent) and narcissistic, given the fact that the two sexual objects were originally the subject itself and the person who first cared for it. In it, Freud identifies a link between the psychic over-evaluation of the sexual object and the idealization of the love-object. In addition, he discusses the fates of primary narcissism with regard to the idealization of the love-object, of the parents as well as with regard to the formation of the Ego Ideal and the idealization of the child to be born. He establishes relationships between the feeling of self-esteem and love life, engages in a discourse on erotic passion and sketches a type of choice of narcissistic object as capable of responding to a "plan for healing neurosis" (choice of therapeutic object).

By defining primary narcissism as an original libidinal investment of the Ego, Freud was indicating that the Ego is in the place of the object and was consequently describing an object-relation.

Instincts and Their Vicissitudes (1915)[9]

In my opinion, the importance of this text especially lies in the following: a synthesis of the characteristics of the sexual drive and its multiple fates; the establishment of an initial drive dualism, Ego drives (self-preservation drives)/sexual drives; an approach to accounting for love and hate, helping us to understand better the elements of hatred present at certain stages in the development of love (oral and anal stages); the notion of affective and drive ambivalence with the masochism/sadism and exhibitionism/voyeurism pairs of opposites.

Observations on Transference-Love (1915)

This remarkable text presents the love experience to us in its natural place, the dual situation. Transference-love is determined by the analytic situation, in which the repetition compulsion solicited leads to the transference and to the theory of object-relations. As Freud wrote:

> It is true that the love consists of new editions of old traits and that it repeats infantile reactions. But this is the essential character of every state of being in love. There is no such state which does not reproduce infantile prototypes.

It is precisely from this infantile determination that it receives its compulsive character, verging as it does on the pathological.[10]

Mourning and Melancholia (*1917*)[11]

Here it is a question of normal and pathological mourning work following a loss of object, of modes of investment of the object and identifications. Freud particularly discussed the problem of identification as being a preliminary stage of object-choice and the first ambivalently expressed way in which the Ego picks out an object (with a desire to incorporate it). He further drew an initial distinction between the narcissistic identification playing a role in melancholic mourning and hysterical identification. This is how he sketched his early ideas about identification, which would be expanded upon in 1921.

Brusset (2007) points out that in this text Freud introduced a considerable change that heralded the second topographical theory and the theory of object-relations.[12] The interchangeable object of the theory of drives has come to play a major role, accounted for by narcissistic investment and ambivalence. Melancholia makes constant aspects of any long-lasting object-relation exemplary: the object, as it manifests itself in clinical practice and in transference, is the site of ambivalent, narcissistic investments, as well being the object of one or another determined drive. But these different aspects neither appear simultaneously, nor on the same level.

Group Psychology and Analysis of the Ego (*1921*)[13]

Apart from Freud's major text on identification – where it is considered to be a primitive form of relationship to the object, but also the fate of the object-relation and where a fundamental dualism between the desire to identify with the object and the desire for a relationship with it, in a complementarity of the roles is observable – the chapter of *Group Psychology and Analysis of the Ego* entitled "Being in Love and Hypnosis"[14] deals with several questions, among them one particularly important for our subject concerning the origin of the lasting investment of the love-object, even in intervals free of sexual desire. He responds to this by combining two currents, tender and sensual, expressed, in terms of drive, by conjoining drives whose goals are inhibited and those that are non-inhibited. Depending on the share enjoyed by tenderness drives, one can measure the intensity of being in love as opposed to purely sexual desire. In another work, *Thoughts for the Times on War and Death* (1915),[15] this intensity of love is explained by that of the counter-investment of unconscious hatred of the object. Freud also moves onto a topographical analysis of being in love by comparing it to hypnosis and the group. He detects an idealization of the object, the object's absorption of the Ego's narcissism, a subsequent impoverishment of the Ego and a diminution of the critical and prohibiting function of the Ego's Ideal. He further establishes differences between identification and being in love, considering all the same that in the latter – even if there is an impoverishment and abandonment of the Ego to the object, put then in place of the Ego's Ideal – there is also an introjection of the object with enrichment of the Ego by the qualities of the latter. Thus, the object would be set in the place of the Ego and/or of the Ego's Ideal.

The Psychogenesis of a Case of Female Homosexuality (1920)[16]

In *The Psychogenesis of a Case of Homosexuality in a Woman*, Freud for the first time brought up another type of object-choice that represents a compromise capable of gratifying heterosexual as well as homosexual desires corresponding to the general bisexuality of human beings. He reminded us in this regard that psychoanalysis had discovered that, alongside their manifest heterosexuality, normal individuals display a very considerable share of latent or unconscious homosexuality. Of the woman's sexuality, he wrote, "Her latest choice corresponded, therefore, not only to her feminine but also to her masculine ideal; it combined satisfaction of the homosexual tendency with that of the heterosexual one."[17] And further on, he added: "In all of us, throughout life, the libido normally oscillates between male and female objects."[18]

Some Neurotic Mechanisms in Jealousy, Paranoia and Homosexuality (1922)[19]

Freud's very illuminating text on jealousy would serve as a reference for Ernest Jones and Melanie Klein. I shall look at this at a later point.

Freud observed that in homosexuality, the separation between social feeling and object-choice is not realized. Furthermore, he pointed out the existence, in principle, of an economic balance between heterosexual investments within the couple and sublimated homosexual investments in the social arena in any subject having attained oedipal organization, something which would be taken up and developed by Catherine Parat in her 1967 report to the congress of romance language psychoanalysts.[20]

The Ego and the Id (1923)[21]

Freud came to the point of envisaging the coexistence in the love relationship of the objectal investment and an identification with the love object, therefore, of Ego and character modification. It is a matter of introjective identification, and the Ego is thus the site of introjected objects. When there is a withdrawal of objectal investment, desexualization takes place leading to identification or to sublimation, accompanied by drive defusion, therefore, by the liberation of the death drive. In this work, Freud also presents a description of the complete Œdipus complex – both positive and negative – with its impact on the love life of the partners, which grows more correspondingly complex. The object-choices (paternal and maternal) lead to identifications and involve two factors of complexity: the triangular arrangement of the oedipal relationship and the individual's constitutional bisexuality. There are two objects, two investments, heterosexual and homosexual, and two drives (Eros and the instinct of destruction). He also brings up the link between ambivalence and bisexuality. The four tendencies are grouped into two identifications, paternal and maternal, so are sexual in nature.

In the second topographical theory, the object plays a major role. In fact, the Ego, the Superego, the Id and the relationships among these different structures within a single personality are constituted during development by the interiorization of relationships with the significant people in one's family circle, objects of desire and objects of identification.

Freud's *The Economic Problem in Masochism* (1924)[22] will be discussed at a later stage in connection with the work of Benno Rosenberg (1991).[23]

Fetishism *(1927)*[24]

In this key text about perversions and their unconscious processes, Freud introduced the dimension of part-objects and of the part-object-relation as they relate to the total object and total object-relation. Set into place are, in particular, fundamental elements of perverted relationships.

The texts on feminine sexuality

In *Some Psychical Consequences of the Anatomical Distinction between the Sexes* (1925),[25] *Female Sexuality* (1931)[26] and "Femininity" (1933),[27] Freud took up the matter of the Œdipus complex in girls, but also of the pre-œdipal mother–child relationship. Indeed, via the Œdipus complex in girls, he led readers to the crucial pre-œdipal period in boys and girls. In girls, there is a necessary change of object, from the mother to the father and a change of erogenous zone, from the clitoris to the vagina. He stressed the girl's attachment to her mother and the importance of the bisexuality of women as compared to that of men. He brings up penis envy in girls and their rejection of femininity. He observed the significant nature of the displacements of the affective and instinctual behavior or motions from the mother to the father, then to the love-object. Women's narcissism would be more marked, with a more distinct desire to be loved, which determines her type of object-choice which is, rather, narcissistic.

Civilization and Its Discontents *(1930)*[28]

Freud understood the psychic experience of the oceanic feeling – which he described as a feeling of infinity, of being limitless, of oneness with the universe – in reference to the most archaic, fetal, symbiotic experience with one's mother. In being in love, he observed that the line of demarcation between the Ego and the object risks being erased, which would correspond to the re-establishment of the limitless narcissism of the first phase of life.

The notion of object-relation and its fates in the hands of different specialists

We cannot envisage the history of the development of the psychoanalytic object that the couple has become without tackling the notion of object-relation and the rich, diverse conceptual elaborations to which it has given rise. As Bernard Brusset has indicated in *Psychanalyse du lien* (2007), the notion of object-relation emerges out of an intellectual movement seeking to free psychoanalysis from certain aspects of Freudian epistemology by re-centering it on the origin and development of objects of love.[29]

Sándor Ferenczi

Brusset sees Sándor Ferenczi as having played a pre-eminent role in the emergence of the above-mentioned movement. In 1909, he began defining the transference by repetition of first object-relations in terms of his theory of primitive introjection. In 1929, his orientation constituted a radical change in psychoanalysis, giving priority to the child's traumatogenic relationships with his or her environment. His famous text "Confusion of tongues between adults and the child" (1931)[30] is exemplary in this regard.

Brusset has detected three major contributions to the theory of object-relation in the legacy of Ferenczi's debate with Freud: those of Alice and Michael Balint, W. R. D. Fairbairn and that of Melanie Klein.

Michael Balint

Michael Balint opened up an entire field of research on the early relations between mother and child. Striving to combine the approaches of Freud and of his own mentor Ferenczi, he adopted positions tending to retain both the theory of drives and that of the object-relation. The choices he made would nevertheless be fairly close to Fairbairn's. The desire for total, unconditional love was the first and most basic form of object-relation. He introduced the notions of "primary love" and "basic fault,"[31] corresponding to shortcomings in the parents and inducing a "basic defect" in the child. For him, the libido presents two basic tendencies: the pursuit of pleasure and of the object. Aggressiveness, as a reaction to the loss of primary love therefore always proves secondary.

William Ronald Dodds Fairbairn

W. R. D. Fairbairn (1889–1964)[32] challenged the exclusively fantasized aspect of object-relation championed by Melanie Klein. Contrary to her, he held that the real object plays a direct decisive role before the internal object is constituted. Ego/object relationships are central and structural in nature. The Ego would in fact be constituted in the very movement by which it invests the object and is fashioned by it. The libido, a function of the Ego, present from the time of birth, is the

18 Some historical points of reference

pursuit of the object and not of pleasure, the latter being but one aspect. The original anxiety would be that of separation with respect to which the interiorization of the object would be a protective measure. Aggression is a reaction to frustration and privation. Finally, he rejected the idea of the existence of a death instinct.

Melanie Klein

Her conception of the object and of the object-relation

Melanie Klein emphasized the fantasized object-relation, therefore, the internal object, whose role is determinant in the processes of projection and introjection of the early stages of development.

The innate destructive drives are constituted right from the time of the child's first experiences as a bad internal object of which it must rid itself, first of all by splitting and projection (paranoid-schizoid position), then by the depressive position, by creating a whole object, both good and bad. The purpose of the depressive position would in fact be the introjection of the good object and the creation of the ambivalent object-relation, meaning the reduction of splittings between good and bad objects, but also between part-objects and whole objects.

The role of the object in the internal world is to differentiate the drives, to organize them. That of the external object would essentially be to limit, to monitor, the system of projection and introjection of bad objects progressively by giving the child sufficiently good experiences, therefore, to manage to correct the projections whose medium it is. Consequently, the parents have a role that tends to be limited to the modulation of the system of projection of internal objects that is progressively rearranged, but not organized, not constituted by them.

Thus, through the quasi-exclusivity given to the economy of internal objects, it would remain very far from the concern to make room for the object's dimension of reality and fundamental alterity.

Love, Hate and Reparation (1937)[33] and Envy and Gratitude (1957)[34]

I have chosen to present these two works that particularly contribute to the understanding of love life and the life of couples. However, I shall only mention the two major texts in which Klein describes the schizo-paranoid and depressive positions, conceptual tools basic to the historical and dynamic comprehension of conjugal ties: "A contribution to the study of the psychogenesis of manic-depressive state" (1934) and "Mourning and its relation to manic-depressive states" (1940).[35]

Klein enriches and deepens certain psychic aspects of love life discovered by Freud. She discusses the ambivalent love/hate conflict as being innate, constitutional. Hate is a destructive, disintegrative force, while love would be a force of harmonization and unification. She differentiates between aggression, the instinct of protection and of struggle for existence and the aggressiveness closely linked

Some historical points of reference   19

to hate. She describes three primitive defense mechanisms in the infant that will be found in love life: projection, the first security measure used by the baby in the face of primordial anxiety represented by the threat of annihilation by the death instinct; the splitting of the world of objects into good and bad, making it possible to avoid the pain of feelings of ambivalence toward one and the same object, the maternal breast, in the first place, then the mother; idealization as a defense against persecution anxiety. The infant's goal would already be to obtain the maximum amount of psychic security and pleasure by making dangerous and destructive feelings disappear. Voracity or the desire to possess would be the expression of the life drive. She describes envy of the other sex: that of the woman with respect to the man would involve the penis, penetration and insemination; that of man with respect to the woman would involve the aptitude for passive experience, the capacity to tolerate, wait and suffer. Following Freud and Ernest Jones, she describes jealousy in love, then genuine love presupposing an aptitude for self-sacrifice, toleration of pain and a certain degree of dependence. As Joan Riviere wrote in their joint book:

> By the partnership in love, therefore, satisfaction of the harmonizing and uni-fying life-instincts, the self-preservative and sexual, is gained; and security against the destructive impulses and dangers of loss, loneliness and helpless-ness is increased. A benign circle of enjoyment with a minimum of privation and aggression has been achieved and the *advantages of dependence* are being used to the full.[36]

Concerning the choice of a love-partner, Melanie Klein reminds us there that the:

> feelings of a man towards a woman are always influenced by his early attach-ment to his mother . . . It is the impression of the loved person that the child had at the time, and the phantasies he connected with her then, which he wishes to rediscover in his later love relationship.[37]

In addition, the unconscious minds of the partners would correspond to one another: the son in the man desires to find the mother and the girl in the woman desires to find the father, which suggests the beginnings of representation of reci-procity in the conjugal relationship.

Looking at the fantasized dimension of male and female sexuality, she especially relates it to diverse sadistic fantasies that the infant directs toward its mother and father. She considers that sexuality is linked to feelings of guilt through the inter-twining of sexual desires and drives of hate and aggressiveness, leading then to a need for reparation with regard to the loved and wounded object. Besides the pleas-ure it affords, sexual gratification also produces a feeling of psychic security and comfort, reassuring the man and woman about the goodness and non-dangerousness of their own, and of their partner's, genitals. So, they are both good, which adds to the genuine sexual enjoyment. Moreover, there would be a desire to identify oneself

20 Some historical points of reference

with both the good parent and the good child, as well as to gratify masculine and feminine desires. The man can share the maternal pleasure of his wife, for example.

On the subject of envy, an important psychic component in the life of couples, Klein's message is rich and invaluable. Occurring right at the beginning of life, this oral-sadistic and anal-sadistic manifestation of destructive drives affects the capacity for sexual enjoyment, which results in gratitude. According to her, penis envy would reflect that of the mother's breast. What is its impact on people's sexual lives?

In women, conquering and collecting men would be a victory over the mother's penis and over her breast. It establishes a link between genital and primary oral gratification.

In men, when envy is too intense, it is in conflict with normal gratification. Hate and anxiety would then be displaced to the vagina. If the oral relation is disturbed, that actually has an impact on their genital relation with women, determining symptoms like impotence, or the compulsive need for genital gratification.

Finally, she reminds us that projective identification and introjective identification are factors contributing to creating confusion, by blurring the boundary lines between the self, on the one hand, and the objects, on the other, between those separating the inner world from the outer world.

Post-Kleinian: Winnicott and Bion

Donald Woods Winnicott and Wilfred Ruprecht Bion would introduce two models of the couple in love, without knowing it: the mother–infant relationship becoming an interrelationship, a "unit," a "couple," and the patient–analyst relationship becoming an analytic couple.

Donald Woods Winnicott

Winnicott presents completely new ideas about the constitution and exploration of the "couple-object in love."

First of all, he discusses the existence, at the beginning of the life of every being, of the "structure, individual–environment organization" unit, the "maternal care–infant" unit,[38] as well as the "mother–child couple" corresponding, according to him, to the primary narcissism underlying the individual's complete fusion in the environment. Between primary narcissism and interpersonal relations, there are intermediary stages represented by objects and transitional phenomena, followed by playing, then later by cultural experience. They are found in a third intermediary area, an area of experience different from psychic reality and external reality, but to which the latter two contribute. This area is located in the variable potential space between the individual and the environment which, in the beginning, joins and separates the baby and its mother, and which "throughout life is retained in the intense experiencing that belongs to the arts and to religion, and imaginative living, and to creative scientific work."[39]

He thus points out to us that the experience common to the members of a group devoting themselves, for example, to religion and to the arts, is made possible by the overlap of personal intermediary areas. Likewise, as another analogy, he proposes psychotherapy, which "takes place in the overlap of two areas of playing, that of the patient and that of the therapist. Psychotherapy has to do with two persons playing together."[40] Would it not be the same within the conjugal couple?

Before taking up creativity and illusion, I would like to mention another invaluable notion that Winnicott has proposed to us: that of interrelationship envisaged in terms of projective and introjective cross-identifications, which presupposes the capacity or incapacity to use projective and introjective mechanisms. So it is, he has explained, that a major part of our life goes on in terms of cross-identifications. It is by "means of cross-identifications that the sharp line of between the me and non-me is blurred."[41] This notion actually leads us to the exploration of certain processes at work in the conjugal relations and their blurring effects on the boundaries between the two 'me's.

Winnicott greatly emphasized the major role played by creativity, to the point of arguing for the existence of an innate creative drive participating in the child's creative potential in connection with illusion, creative life and the fact of living. He even discusses "the infant's ability to use *illusion* without which no contact is possible between the psyche and the environment,"[42] and the fact that "if we wish we may collect together and form a group on the basis of our illusory experiences."[43] Creation, he maintained, is determined by the impulse of need and of drive and illusion. It is believing that what the child has created has a real existence.

These notions associated with those of innate potential for growth and development, of maturational processes, could also help us envisage another analogy, that of every young couple to an infant, a living being in a process of becoming, full of creative potentialities, of growth, integration and maturation.

Among these maturational processes, in both the child and the couple, the depressive position seems to me to be fundamental. Winnicott has described it as corresponding to the stage of concern, with tolerated ambivalence, feelings of guilt and reparation, giving, offering, caring for the other person, feelings of personal responsibility. According to him, feelings of guilt flow from a personal source that starts with the joining of two mothers, those of calm love and of excited love, those of love and of hate.

The development of the capacity for concern (1962)[44] is an important feature of social life. The simultaneous experience of love and hate leads to the success of ambivalence, then its enrichment and its refinement lead to the manifestation of concern.

Bisexuality as a quality of the "total self" is also a major notion Winnicott offers us. The pure female and male elements, the experience of being, based on that of omnipotence, enabling the establishment of a sense of Self, a subject/object non-drive identity, on the one hand, and, on the other hand, the doing and the drive object relation presupposing the subject/object separation,[45] could constitute two poles around which the groupal (pure female) and intersubjective (pure male) conjugal dynamic would be structured and oscillate – the combination of the two realizing a "conjugal total self" expressing its bisexuality.

Finally, I would like to draw attention to Winnicott's paper "Communicating and non-communicating" (1963), in which he wrote that *"each individual is an isolate, permanently non-communicating, permanently unknown, in fact unfound,"* at the center of which is an incommunicado element, the self's core, the secret self, that is not supposed to communicate with the world of perceived objects.[46] Within the couple, there would also be zones of non-communication. Thus, communication would neither be total, nor ongoing, which leads me conclude this overview of Winnicott's contributions to the construction and intelligibility of the conjugal couple with his article "The capacity to be alone" (1958), which is about "the foundation on which sophisticated aloneness is built." The capacity to be alone depends on the existence of good internal objects, on good internalized relationships in the psychic reality of the individual providing a feeling of confidence about the present and the future and relative freedom from persecutory anxiety. Winnicott explains that:

> Being alone in the presence of someone, can take place at a very early stage, when the *ego immaturity is naturally balanced by ego-support* from the mother. In the course of time the individual introjects the ego-supportive mother and in this way becomes able to be alone without frequent reference to the mother or mother symbol.

The individual establishes "an internal environment." Winnicott further suggests that it "could be said that the individual's capacity to be alone depends on his ability to deal with the feelings aroused by the primal scene."[47]

What about aloneness and this individual "capacity to be alone" in the psychic presence of another person within a couple?

Wilfred Ruprecht Bion

Bion has made numerous contributions:

- through his innovative research on the dynamics of small groups, with the processes and formations specific to them, which would be one of the origins of the psychoanalytic approach to groups;
- through his exploration of the mother–infant relationship and the patient–analyst relationship, both conceived of as interrelationships, and no longer as unilateral object-relations.

Let us take up his innovative contributions for psychoanalytic understanding of groups, which would, on the one hand, have a determinant impact on studies undertaken by the British, Argentine and French schools, and which, on the other hand, for me represent one of the essential milestones in the constitution of this couple-object, conceived of as a natural group.

A psychoanalytic understanding of groups

To begin with, Bion considers that the individual is and always has been a member of a group, a "group animal" in conflict, with both the group and the aspects of his or her own personality constituting his or her "groupishness." In this respect, he is unlike Freud who, according to him, "limits this war to a struggle with 'culture'."[48] These notions of "groupishness" and of every individual's groupal belonging seem to me to be fundamental and particularly new.

Bion wrote that "no individual, however isolated in time and space, can be regarded as outside a group or lacking in active manifestations of group psychology."[49] Later on, he added that "the apparent difference between group psychology and individual psychology is an illusion produced by the fact that the group brings into prominence phenomena that appear alien to an observer unaccustomed to using the group."[50]

In connection with the "groupishness" of every individual, Bion introduced the notion of "group mentality" independent of individual mentality. For him, this was what consolidates the group, but also what keeps it from working. I shall come back to this. First, I need to discuss what Bion defined as "the phantasy that the group exists." He has written:

> Substance is given to the phantasy that the group exists by the fact that the regression involves the individual in a loss of his "individual distinctiveness" . . . indistinguishable from depersonalization, and therefore obscures observation that the aggregate is of individuals. It follows that, if the observer judges a group to be in existence, the individuals composing it must have experienced this regression.[51]

In addition, Bion detected in every group the existence of a plurality of conflicting trends of mental activity, principally represented by the "work group" and the "basic group" based on "basic assumptions."

It would be a matter of two modes of psychic functioning in small groups. The work group represents conscious, voluntary cooperation on the part of the members in engaging in an activity oriented toward a common task in relationship to reality. It would involve the characteristics of the Ego and would be driven by logic of the functioning of secondary psychic processes. Nevertheless, this conscious cooperation on the part of the members of the group is not exclusively rational, "made secondary," but is also driven by an unconscious fantasized, emotional flow that is at times paralyzing, at times stimulating. The basic group manifests itself in this way with its logic of the functioning of the primary psychic processes. According to Bion, the individuals assembled in a group instantaneously and involuntarily enter into combination ("valency")[52] so

24 Some historical points of reference

as to act in accordance with the emotional states that Bion calls "basic assumptions." He identifies three such assumptions (dependence, fight–flight, pairing) which alternate in dominating a group without the group recognizing them. They do not appear at the same time. One is dominant and obscures the others, which remain virtual, constituting the "proto-mental system."

These three basic assumptions characterizing the different possible contents of the group mentality would correspond, according to Bion, to defensive groupal reactions to the psychotic anxieties reactivated by the regression imposed upon the individual in the group situation.

This is why Bion, inspired by Klein and unlike Freud, who had identified neurotic mechanisms within groups – family groups as well as specialized groups like the Church and the army – actually detected and explored a level of functioning and psychotic mechanisms belonging to schizo-paranoid and depressive positions that seemed to him to play the central role.

The mother–infant and patient–analyst interrelationships

Following Melanie Klein, Bion accorded prime importance to the projective identification associated with the mother's capacity for reverie or with that of the analyst, factor of the alpha-function. He also introduced the container/contained relationship, implicit in the processes of projective identification.

Genetic links exist between thought and projective identification, Bion thought. Indeed, intolerance of frustration determines increased tension of/in the mental apparatus. Thought would originally be a process of discharging the mental apparatus of increased tension, with projective identification being a mechanism based on the "omnipotent fantasy that it is possible to split off temporarily undesired, though sometimes valued, parts of the personality, and put them in an object," which therefore presupposes the correlative existence of a container in which a contained is projected and of a contained that can be projected into the container.[53]

What about the mother's capacity for reverie?

"For example," Bion explains, "when the mother loves the infant, what does she do it with? Leaving aside the physical channels of communication, my impression is that her love is expressed by reverie."[54] This would consist of transforming a sensory experience into a psychic, emotional experience. This transformation presupposes a mode of projection of raw, unintegratable containeds, the beta-elements, whose treatment by the other person, (mother, analyst) – through metabolization, detoxification, elaboration, connected with their capacity for reverie – makes re-introjection possible. Bion explains that this "maternal alpha-function" "becomes introjected by the infant so that the . . . apparatus becomes installed in the infant as part of the apparatus of alpha-function."[55] It is a matter of the container/contained system at work from that time on in the infant. The same would be true in the patient–analyst relationship.

So, this is what I shall retain of Bion's contribution to the construction of the couple-object.

Henry Dicks and Jürg Willi

By introducing the notion of "collusion," Dicks and Willi offer us a new picture of the intersubjective, conjugal relationship, which is now systemic and dynamic, animated by structuring unconscious processes.

Henry V. Dicks: **Marital Tensions** *(1967)*[56]

Heir to Klein's and Fairbairn's legacy, Dicks would introduce the notion of "collusion." He emphasized the ambivalent ties by means of which a subject chooses in his or her partner a certain manner of reacting to what he or she has repressed in him or her. According to Dicks, this initial attraction will later become the origin of crisis between the partners if one partner's intrapsychic conflicts, being in resonance with their repression in the other, reactivates that structured collusion owing to an interplay of projections and introjections, essentially projective identifications. This collusion is remarkable in that it especially uses what Dicks calls "floating projections" between the two partners, each one seeking protection by projecting different aspects of "internalized bad objects" onto the other.

Jürg Willi: **Couples in Collusion** *(1975)*[57]

Jürg Willi would expand upon the notion of collusion introduced by Dicks to make it a central concept accounting for certain aspects of the unconscious intersubjective dimension of couples. This would be taken up by Jean-Georges Lemaire.

Under the influence of Dicks, Willi called *collusion* the partners' common game on the basis of this common unconscious (basic theme common to both partners and implicit in the conjugal conflict).

Indeed, according to Willi, the two partners share unresolved common unconscious conflictual problems, which constitute the object of their mutual attraction – and therefore of their "dyadic conflict" – but also would prove to be a source of the conflicts that would later arise and seek resolution in their couple through a distribution of ("progressive" or "regressive") complementary "defensive" roles. Each partner would thus feel his or her defensive system reinforced by his or her partner. However, after some period of their life together, this "collusive attempt at healing" is thwarted by the return of the repressed, that of the derivatives of the unconscious and certain aspects already displaced (delegated out or externalized) onto the partner surface anew from each partner's Ego.

As a consequence, Willi envisages the choice of partner as a compromise formation and the conjugal conflict as a common neurotic symptom. He then detects four basic types of collusion:

- "Narcissistic collusion" is characterized by the bond between two partners, one of whom, narcissistic, embodies his or her Ego Ideal for the other, nurturing then his or her narcissism with the idealization necessary to the partner with the weak Ego. Dissimulated in both is nostalgia for the total symbiosis to which their love relationship aspires.

- "Oral collusion" revolves around the theme of love assimilated to a mother–child relationship. To love is to procure care, concern, protection and subsistence for oneself. The relationship is characterized by the role of mother played by one of the partners, while the other plays the role of child. One will give and the other receive. This is their basic premise. The "child" presses the partner to maintain concern and the "mother" presses the other person to regress in the need for help.
- In "anal–sadistic collusion," Willi differentiates between dominant–dominated, sado-masochist, and jealousy–infidelity collusion. Thus, the "active" partner tends toward domination, autonomy and infidelity, repressing, then delegating to the partner, his or her desires for submission, dependence and separation anxiety. The "passive" partner tends toward dependence, submission and jealousy, and thus represses, delegates, desires for autonomy, but also fantasies of infidelity to the partner.
- "phallic–œdipal collusion" finds expression in a set of problems involving the masculine role played within the couple and in the rivalry between the two partners in this domain. The man will tend to maintain a virile attitude, but will repress and delegate his feminine passive tendencies to his partner. The partner will tend to accept the feminine passive position, but will also repress and delegate to her partner her aspirations to make virile, phallic claims.

Furthermore, participating in the structuring of all conjugal life, the Œdipus complex will also orient the choice of partner, and the non-resolution of the œdipal conflict may, according to Willi, represent an obstacle to the constitution of a couple, out of fear of incest, especially.

He points out that it is only a matter of dynamic principles. Moreover, he considers that in every conjugal relationship, each of the partners is faced with these issues, both their regressive aspect and their progressive aspect. The essential criterion for a healthy relationship would lie in the flexibility with which each partner can play the roles, at times regressive, at times progressive, while the pathological relationship would be marked by rigidity and a defensive fixity of the roles of each party.

Apart from this interesting theoretical elaboration of collusion as an unconscious neurotic game common to both partners of the couple or the "common unconscious," Willi also indicates to us that in the conjugal relationship, certain character traits are strengthened, while others become less significant, being capable of determining a new facet of the personality, just as a more or less significant part of the relational potential proper to each partner may not form part of the couple, but may be realized in other areas: the subject's fantasized universe, family, professional and social life, and, finally, leisure activities, especially.

This raises some fundamental questions: What portion of every subject's psyche would be mobilized in conjugal life? What effect would the couple have on the unconscious psychic life of each of the partners? What about the different types and varied modes of psychic functioning in accordance with the relational fields and sensitivities invested by every subject?

Jean-Georges Lemaire

Seminal studies and conceptions of the couple

Allow me to cite Jean-Georges Lemaire's seminal writings: *Les conflits conjugaux* (Conjugal Conflicts) (1966); *Les thérapies du couple* (Couple Therapies) (1971); *Le couple: sa vie, sa mort* (The Couple: Its Life and Its Death) (1979); *Famille, amour, folie* (Family, Love, Madness) (1989); *Les mots du couple* (The Couple's Words) (1998); *Comment faire avec la passion* (What to Do with Passion) (2005); and a collective work, *L'inconscient dans la famille* (The Unconscious in the Family) (2007).[58]

Lemaire founded the French association of centers of conjugal consultation (AFCCC) in 1961. He created the journal *Dialogue* in 1963 and then the center for training in therapies for couples and families (PSYFA) in 1979.

He would approach the strictly intersubjective dimension of the couple, synchronic as well as diachronic, from a twofold perspective, psychoanalytic and systemic. He would take up the notion of collusion elaborated by Willi, would use Freudian, Kleinian and Winnicottian notions and concepts to make the choice of spouse, the phases of the life of the couple, the phenomena of conjugal conflict and crisis intelligible. He would also be sensitive to the characteristics of the pregenital object-relations explored by Maurice Bouvet. Moreover, he would rely upon concepts derived from communication theory, itself centered on the system model and its principles of structuring, functioning and regulation. Finally, he has more recently explored the pragmatic aspects of verbal and non-verbal language.

So it is that he conceives of the couple as a human micro-group organized into a structured, self-regulated system, based on the interaction of each individual's conscious and unconscious desires and needs, and on an intense, ambivalent mutual investment. This structured whole is patterned by alternations of organization, disorganization and reorganization of processes and phases of the interrelationships between the partners, producing a balance that is dynamic in nature. But he also envisages the couple as an interplay of projections and of introjective and projective identifications between the partners lending their couple a long-lasting, stable form.

With regard to heterosexual couples, he distinguishes love affairs (short-term couples) from what are called conjugal couples (long-term couples).

In the short-term couple, what is expected of the partner is above all rapid, tangible satisfaction of a libidinal and/or narcissistic kind. The pursuit of pleasure is evident through the quest for the object, the pleasure of conquest, confirmation of the ability to seduce. If there is no longer any gratification of this nature the ties disappear.

28 Some historical points of reference

A long-term couple is one having an implicit or explicit family project. While the object must also provide libidinal and narcissistic satisfactions, it is integrated into the subject's defensive organization against a rejected, repressed part of him- or herself. Therefore, the internalized object in love is used as a means of defense by the subject, whence comes a more intense, more possessive bond with the object, since it is through this more or less reciprocal possession of the other person that a defense mechanism is put into place.

I shall return to Lemaire's major contribution in Chapter 4 on the natural history of the couple, especially as it concerns modes of structuring the couple, therefore, of different types of choices of partner, as well as the beginnings of the couple's natural history and later crisis phenomena. Finally, I shall discuss certain of his ideas in Chapter 6, devoted to therapeutic work.

Group psychoanalysis and its impact in France

The emergence of the groupal psychoanalytic model with its diverse variants represents an epistemological innovation in the history of the construction of our couple-object. Indeed, from the psychoanalytic approaches to the instinctual, fantasized, affective "object-relations" aspects of love life, my research has evolved in the direction of the intersubjective, interrelational dimension made conceivable by using mother–infant and patient–analyst relationship models developed by Winnicott and Bion. Then, with the introduction of the concept of collusion by Dicks, developed by Willi and finally Lemaire's theories, I have come to understand the couple in its twofold dimension: intersubjective, defensive in particular and systemic. This is why I consider that this groupal model will both provide a representation of the couple and its psychic reality unprecedented up until then, and lay the foundations for a different type of psychotherapeutic technique for conjugal groups.

In Argentina

Enrique Pichon-Rivière (1965)[59] developed an understanding of groups marked by a socio-analytic psychology. José Bleger (1967)[60] established a fundamental distinction between two forms of sociability: synchretic and through interaction.

In Great Britain

S. H. Foulkes, J. Rickman and Henry Ezriel[61] laid the foundations of group analysis in London at the beginning of the 1940s. Broadly speaking, this is a method of investigating the psychic formations and processes that develop in a group. It bases its concepts and its technique upon certain fundamental facts of psychoanalytic theory and method, and upon original psychoanalytic studies required by taking the group into consideration as a specific entity. In a narrower sense, group analysis is a technique of group psychotherapy and a device for psychoanalytic experimentation with the unconscious in group situations.

Some historical points of reference   29

In the same hospital as Foulkes, Bion would propose a different original conception of group formations and processes.

In France

Beginning in the mid-1960s, criticizing the direct application of psychoanalytic concepts deriving from the individual course of treatment to the group, Didier Anzieu, Angélo Bejarano and Jean-Bertrand Pontalis, then René Kaës proposed a different psychoanalytic approach to groups.

Jean-Bertrand Pontalis and the small group as object (1963)[62]

According to Pontalis, the group functions as a fantasy in the individual psyche. It therefore restores to the group its value as a psychic object, as a drive investment and as unconscious representations for its subjects. According to René Kaës, Pontalis' study of the small group as object marked a turning point in French group psychoanalysis.

Didier Anzieu, the dream model (1966) and his book The Group and the Unconscious (1975)[63]

Groups, like dreams, are a means of fulfilling unconscious wishes. So it is that Anzieu proposed a model for understanding groups as entities within which unconscious processes operate that is in line with Bion's and Foulkes' approaches, but uses the dream model.

Furthering Bion's ideas, Anzieu considered that groups function on two levels, which they tend to keep separate, that of fantasized activity and that of the work group. Indeed, the members of a group come together to accomplish a common task. But any interhuman bond would result from a fantasized flow between the members, who produce compromise formations, such as ideologies, mythologies and utopias. On the fantasized level, a group experiences itself as a living body, to borrow a biological metaphor, each participant of which recognizes him- or herself as member. There would be a desire for a "group Self" to take up residence in a living organism.

Anzieu detected five unconscious psychic group organizers:

- Individual fantasy, combined with the phenomenon of fantasized resonance described by André Missenard (1971) and taken up again by Anzieu as being the grouping of certain participants around one of them who, through his or her acts, way of being or remarks, has displayed or communicated one of his or her unconscious individual fantasies. Grouping means interest, convergence, feedback, mutual stimulation.[64] The instigator of the fantasy is then placed in the position of groupal Ego. Finally, its origin would be found in the symbiotic, dual relationship between the child and its mother.

30 Some historical points of reference

- The imagos;
- Primal fantasies;
- The Œdipus complex, as meta-organizer;
- The body image and psychic envelope of the groupal apparatus.

Thus, the leader, the group, the ideology, will come to replace an agency itself in the psychic apparatuses of the members. On the other hand, their function is to contain the unconscious psychic processes occurring among the members. The dominant structure in the groupal apparatus would become the envelope (leader, ideology).

Furthermore, the groupal fantasized life would flow out of three principles of psychic functioning proper to the groupal apparatus:

- a principle of non-differentiation of the individual and the group;
- a principle of self-sufficiency of the group in relationship to physical and social reality;
- a principle of delimitation between something inside the group and the outside.

Anzieu maintained that the modes of thought and action, the perceptions of reality, are infiltrated by prevalent individual fantasies emanating from certain members and developing symptoms of contagion or resistance in others. Thus, the convergence of fantasies and their unifying creation can give birth to a well-defined, specific, ideology or mythology.

René Kaës (2007, 2009)[65]

The psychoanalytic approach to groups has enabled Kaës to discern three logical levels in the study of this reality: that of the group; that of the bonds among the subjects making up the group; and that of each subject considered in his or her singularity. Kaës thinks that the group experience is essentially one of assembling or fitting together these three spaces (group, intersubjective bonds and intrapsychic space). It was in order to think through these relations that at the end of the 1960s, he proposed a model – that of the *groupal psychic apparatus* – capable of accounting for these three spaces and their assemblage. He would thus enable psychoanalytic knowledge to extend to the "psychic consistency" of each of these three spaces and to that of the processes and formations uniting them and separating them.

Moreover, a certain number of notions and concepts also helped him to think through these multiple relations, among them: the notion of internal groups and the concept of psychic groupality, phoric functions, common and shared oneiric space, unconscious alliances and intersubjective work, especially.

The *internal groups* (primary and secondary) are groups situated within ourselves, "we are a group." The primary groups, in particular, encompass the network of identifications, the groupal structure of the Ego, the group of object-relations, oedipal and sibling complexes and the body image. *Psychic groupality* is that general property of psychic matter that is associating, undoing, leveling psychic objects, forming assemblages out of them in keeping with laws of composition and of transformation as a result of the act of life and death instincts, as a result of repression or mechanisms without repression, by splitting, denial or rejection.[66] By this groupality, we become "plural singular" subjects.

This concept of internal groupality gives us part of the answer to the question of how subjects form a group. Indeed, internal groups would function as psychic organizers of the group in combination with socio-cultural organizers. Thus, each group would be characterized by a pair of predominant socio-cultural and psychic organizers from which its identity and the identifications of its members are stabilized.

Consequently, Kaës envisages the mobilization of these two series of organizers in the processes of fitting psyches together by the groupal apparatus, as well as certain necessary requirements of psychic work, several sets of processes and of the modes of fitting them together.

He also introduces the notion of *phoric functions*. Indeed, he has observed that certain subjects perform intermediary, coordinating functions within the group, within the transitions between each subject's psychic spaces and the common, shared psychic spaces (couple, group, family, institution). The persons embodying them bear these functions as much as they are borne by them. They are the message-bearers, the symptom-bearers, the bearers of ideals, etc. What is rightly incumbent upon the subject in the function that he or she is performing and what is assigned to him or her in this function by the groupal processes?

Kaës then identifies several characteristics common to these functions, among them: the functions of delegation, of representation and transmission, as well as of containing, semiotization and symbolization.

What about *unconscious alliances*? Kaës calls an unconscious alliance, an intersubjective psychic formation constructed by subjects who are involved in a bond in order to strengthen in each of them and to establish at the basis of their bond the narcissistic, objectal investments they need, the processes, the functions and the psychic structures necessary to them that have come from repression, or denial, rejection and disavowal. The alliance is formed in such a way that the bond takes on decisive psychic value for each of its subjects The assemblage bound together in this way (the group, the family, the couple) takes its psychic reality from the alliances, contracts and pacts that its subjects conclude and that their place in the assemblage obliges them to maintain.[67]

But, unconscious alliances have another dimension, which concerns each subject involved in them. They require obligations and subjugation of them. They confer benefits upon them. But above all, they fashion part of the unconscious and of the psychic reality of each subject.

Kaës discerns three categories of them: structuring, defensive and offensive. Unconscious structuring alliances contribute to the structuring of the psyche, such as: the œdipal pact concluded with the father (symbolic contract) and among siblings; the contract of mutually renouncing the direct realization of destructive instinctual goals, condition for the coming of the community of law; narcissistic pacts and contracts. Defensive alliances especially include the denegative pact, but also their pathological

32 Some historical points of reference

and alienating excesses, among them the community of denial and perverted contract. The offensive alliances seal the agreement of a group to lead an attack, engage in an exploit or exercise supremacy. I shall return to this in a later chapter.

The concepts of unconscious alliances and of phoric functions, in particular, present a twofold subjective and intersubjective valence and a twofold metapsychological affiliation. We could understand them in terms of an intersubjective topographical economy and dynamic.

Kaës discusses, in addition, the intersubjectivity that imposes psychic work upon psyche owing to the subject's necessary intersubjective situation, which leads him or her to conceive the concept of *intersubjectivity work*, psychic work of the unconscious of the other person or of more than one other person in the psyche of the subject of the unconscious.

Consequently, the psychic space of the bond and that of the assemblages are other sites of the unconscious and, according to him, the psychoanalytic work in group situations has modified the traditional conception of the unconscious psychic conflict. Indeed, besides the intrapsychic conflict of infantile psychosexual, therefore neurotic, origin there would be an unconscious conflict between the subject and the part of his or her psyche held by another person (or more than one other person) or left in him or her (in them). Of course, the exploration of the "borderline cases" has also revealed the existence of another type of unconscious conflict, that between the Ego and its objects.

I consider this theoretical contribution deriving from Kaës' work to be significant and particularly invaluable for developing a metapsychological understanding of couples.

Some contemporary French conceptions

How have contemporary psychoanalysts of couples used these notions and concepts elaborated by group analysts? In response to that question, I have chosen to present the ideas of Jean-Pierre Caillot and Gérard Decherf, of Albert Eiguer, and then those of André Ruffiot. Finally, I shall add my own.

Psychoanalysis of the Couple and of the Family (1989) by Jean-Pierre Caillot and Gérard Decherf [68]

Jean-Pierre Caillot and Gérard Decherf have taken up the notions of groupality and group-object, and use the latter to define the existence of a family-object, meaning of a fantasy of the family as object, in the sense of a correlate of drives, established as a prototype of group-objects. The couple-object would be the unitary representation of the couple that has an imaginary common body and an imaginary common psyche. According to these specialists, the couple's functioning is characterized by the fact that it is invested as an object, whether it is a matter of the internal object or of the external object. Via fantasized resonance, the couple's psychic apparatus would form by connecting together individual psychic apparatuses.

And this connecting is established and develops in a common fantasized space, intermediary between the couple as external object and the two members' internal couple-objects. It is within this space that the common formations, of the ideal and of the superego, are going to be produced and transformed. They introduce, moreover, interesting notions for family and conjugal clinical work, those of anti-family couple and anti-couple family, in particular.

Alberto Eiguer: psychoanalytic therapy of couples, Psychoanalytic Work with Couples[69]

For Alberto Eiguer, couples combine two types of bonds, object libidinal and narcissistic, and two "forces" would make it possible to situate conjugal conflicts: rapprochement anxiety and the conflict between two narcissisms leading to non-recognition of the spouse's specific character and alterity.

He has defined the notion of the couple's "permanent structure" as represented by a mode of unconscious conflict between groupal structures and by a specific mode of collective fantasies. The structure itself would be defined from the economic, dynamic, topical and genetic viewpoints. He borrows the concept of unconscious psychic organizer and applies it to the couple, taking an interest in mechanisms that lend a couple its cohesiveness. He detects three of these within the couple's unconscious life and notes how each one structures each type of couple: *the object-choice*; *the conjugal Self*, with its three components (joint feeling of belonging, internal habitat and Ideal of the conjugal Ego). Indeed, the couple structures its narcissistic bonds on this organizing structure defined as the representation, shared by the partners, of their couple, in spatio-temporal continuity. He establishes parallels between *interfantasizing* and the concept of "fantasized collusion" introduced by Dicks[70] and expanded upon by Willi and then Lemaire. The different components of conjugal Self would be the reflection of this interfantasizing as the references to the lineage shared by the partners and the mythopoeic activity flowing out of it. Very active at the time of the love commitment, it determines the couple's typical structure and is at the origin of the conflictual mode. It is the site of the meeting of each partner's individual unconscious fantasies.

He defined four types of couples in terms of these three organizers and their variable forms: normal or neurotic, anaclitic or depressive, narcissistic and perverted. He thus observed convergences with the typology proposed by Willi.

Finally, Eiguer inquired into the presence of the transgenerational and the modes according to which the transgenerational representations connected with ancestors circulate in couples.

André Ruffiot

André Ruffiot was one of the pioneers of the psychoanalysis of the couple and of the family in France. His early works include: *L'instinct du couple* (The Couple

34 Some historical points of reference

Instinct) (1972); *Mélanie Klein et le couple* (Melanie Klein and the Couple) (1974); *Le Soi Conjugal* (The Conjugal Self) (1975).

I shall present some of his major ideas as expressed in a collection of writings on the *psychoanalytic therapy of couples* published in 1984.[71]

Ruffiot conceives of the psychic dyad as possessing all the characteristics of a supra-individual psyche endowed with its own topography and having a dynamic and an economy completely specific to it.

- On the topographical level, the couple-object would fulfill the function of transindividual psyche, extra-territorial structure, where the couple-subject is indistinguishable from the couple-object.
- The dyadic dynamic would be characterized by diverse types of conflict: that concerning the couple's relationships and boundaries with "external world" and, within the couple, those inherent in the "inter-narcissistic confrontation" and the difference between the sexes.
- The dyadic economy is characterized by an exchange and a regulation of the psychic energy ensuring the couple's long-lastingness and by a specific economic regime involving the pooling of the individual Ids and an ongoing re-energizing of the Egos. Mutually invested objects and other objects invested separately would exist.

According to Ruffiot, love would fit into a category analogous to that of the originary. He identified characteristics common to those two categories. So it is that love work would consist of fitting what is corporally well-tried and the other person's body into one's own psyche. There would also be the work of fitting two distinct bodies into a dual psyche, unified in its functioning.

He considered groupality to be at the basis of the human group and unconscious group fantasizing to be at the heart of love. Indeed, beyond the œdipal connotations and the desire for identification with the mother and with her creative powers, the love desire would also involve a fantasy of giving birth. The love fantasy contains a family fantasy. Marriage would be the social revealing and legitimization by the group of sexual exchanges that had remained intimate and discreet up until that point, something which underscores the couple's desire to fit into the social group also.

Finally, he discussed conjugal crisis. If the love phenomenon is "the normal prototype of psychosis," the conjugal crisis establishes in the dyad a kind of mental functioning possessing all psychotic virtualities with mechanisms of denial, split between good object/bad object, good Ego/bad Ego, accompanied by a paranoid experience of the internalized partner and felt as a part of the Ego placing individual intactness in danger. The love-object would be an internal persecutor.

My view of the couple

For me, the couple is a historically and socio-culturally determined, living and composite – sexual-bodily, socio-cultural and psychic – reality with diverse and variable interrelationships. It involves several ambivalently transferential figures playing multiple roles within this inter-transferential dynamic organization determined by a compulsion for repetition of "infantile prototypes." Inspired by Freud on the subject of analytic transference, I maintain that the couple creates and constitutes an *inter-transferential neurosis*, while nevertheless presenting psychotic virtualities, in particular during critical periods and events, that then reactivate each one of the partners' depressive and paranoid-schizophrenic positions. This inter-transferential neurosis unfolds and evolves in accordance with a complicated temporality combining historical and socio-cultural, bodily and psychic temporality, the latter being multiple, composed of progressive, regressive movements, fixations, repetition compulsion, but also of after effects. In addition, every couple's becoming is inevitably regularly marked by mutative and maturing critical stages. *Ambivalently invested, the couple is then structurally and dynamically as conflictual as it is critical.*

The couple's sexual-bodily reality involves two human beings, and their sexual bodies, as well as two "psychosomatic organizations" living together with implicit or explicit plans "to reproduce," thus participating in the vast program of preservation of the species. It is a matter, therefore, of a biological unit of procreation. These two sexual bodies and "psychosomatic organizations" communicate with one another in accordance with varied verbal and non-verbal modes: mimetic-gestural, behavioral, fantasized and sexual. Vis-à-vis the other person's body there are: reciprocal flows of drive investments (narcissistic, erotic, tender and aggressive); representations (conscious, preconscious and unconscious); and projective and identificatory movements mobilizing the psychic bisexuality of each partner, which participate in the elaboration of a "psycho-bodily pairing," or rather of a "fantasy of psycho-bodily pairing."

For its part, the sexual act would, in particular, realize the group fantasy of an "imaginary common body," a bisexual, unconscious, fantasized body. Moreover, it actualizes the regressive desire for narcissistic union, conferring upon both a state of narcissistic completeness.

Its socio-cultural reality is characterized by the presence of two individuals living together and constituting a social unit of economic production and cooperation, of social reproduction and of child raising, for the couple that has become parental. Inspired by Bion ("work group") 1953,[72] I see them as forming a *work couple* ensuring its material means of existence. Finally, they belong to a social group, occupy a position in the social structure and are endowed with roles and functions. Their couple can be institutionalized by marriage as well as by other forms of social recognition. They thereby elaborate together a conjugal "culture" and "identity."

Finally, its *psychic reality* consists of fundamental psychic components ensuring its "psychic consistency,"[73] made up, notably, of a plurality of conflictualities, of flows of drive investments, of fantasies of desire, of object-relations, of an interplay of identifications and of projections, imagos, anxieties and multiple correlative defense mechanisms applied in the structuring and functioning of this conjugal dyad.

36 Some historical points of reference

Inspired by Kaës' 2007 work *Un singulier pluriel*,[74] I envisage three "logical levels" in my approach to the conjugal psychic reality:

- The group level, common psychic reality shared by its members, with its specific organizers and its formations.
- The level of the intersubjective relationship, with its modalities and variable levels of object-relations, its unconscious alliances (structuring, defensive, even offensive), the relating of Œdipus and sibling complexes, especially. The triangulation secured within the intersubjective love relationship by the co-creation of the conjugal group, common, shared fantasized living being and psychic cradle of the future child to be born would contribute to the consolidation of the partners' oedipal organization.
- The intrapsychic-individual level, with its own conflicts between the Ego and its internal love-object (trauma-object, following André Green, 1983),[75] between its two specific psychic objects, the love-object and the couple-object, but also in the Ego's tense relationship with the couple-group, between the similitude and difference of psychic spaces.

This conjugal, historical reality is also alive with multiple conflictualities and antagonisms, both internal and external, that are in an ongoing relationship of tension with one another. I shall expand upon this more at a later point.

Notes

1 Bernard Brusset (2007), *Psychanalyse du lien*. Paris: Presses universitaires de France.
2 Sigmund Freud (1905), *Three Essays on the Theory of Sexuality. S.E.*7. London: Hogarth.
3 Sigmund Freud (1912), *On the Universal Tendency to Debasement in the Sphere of Love. S.E.* 11, London: Hogarth, pp. 177–90.
4 *Ibid.* p. 183.
5 *Ibid.*, pp. 186–7.
6 *Ibid*, pp. 185–6.
7 Sigmund Freud (1918a), *The Taboo of Virginity. S.E.* 11, London: Hogarth, pp. 191–208.
8 Sigmund Freud (1914a), *On Narcissism: An Introduction. S.E.*, 14. London: Hogarth.
9 Sigmund Freud (1915c), *Instincts and Their Vicissitudes. S.E.*, 14. London: Hogarth.
10 Sigmund Freud (1915a), *Observations on Transference-Love, S.E.*, 12. London: Hogarth, p. 168.
11 Sigmund Freud (1917), *Mourning and Melancholia. S.E.*, 14, London: Hogarth, pp. 237–8.
12 *Op. cit.*, Brusset.
13 Sigmund Freud (1921), *Group Psychology and the Analysis of the Ego. S.E.*, 18, London: Hogarth.
14 *Ibid.*, Chapter VIII.
15 Sigmund Freud (1915b), *Thoughts for the Times on War and Death. S.E.*, 14, London: Hogarth.
16 Sigmund Freud, (1920), *The Psychogenesis of a Case of Female Homosexuality. S.E.*, 18, London: Hogarth.
17 *Ibid.*, p. 156.

Some historical points of reference 37

18 *Ibid.*, p. 158.
19 Sigmund Freud (1922), *Some Neurotic Mechanisms in Jealousy, Paranoia and Homosexuality, S.E.*, 18, London: Hogarth.
20 Catherine Parat (1967), "L'organisation œdipienne du stade genital, Rapport au congrès des psychanalystes de langues françaises," *Revue française de psychanalyse*, vol. 31, no. 5–6 (September–December).
21 Sigmund Freud (1923), *The Ego and the Id. S.E.*, 19. London: Hogarth.
22 Sigmund Freud (1924a), *The Economic Problem of Masochism. S.E.*, 19, London: Hogarth.
23 Benno Rosenberg (1991), *Masochisme gardien de la vie, masochisme mortifère*. Paris: Presses universitaires de France.
24 Sigmund Freud (1927), *Fetishism. S.E.* 21, London: Hogarth.
25 Sigmund Freud (1925), *Some Psychical Consequences of the Anatomical Distinction between the Sexes. S.E.*, 19. London: Hogarth.
26 Sigmund Freud (1931), *Female Sexuality. S.E.*, 21, London: Hogarth.
27 Sigmund Freud (1933), *Femininity. Lecture XXXIII of New Introductory Lectures. S.E.*, 22, London: Hogarth.
28 Sigmund Freud (1930), *Civilization and Its Discontents. S.E.*, 21. London: Hogarth.
29 *Op. cit.* Brusset, p. 70.
30 Sándor Ferenczi (1931), Confusion of tongues between adults and the child (1933). In: *Final Contributions to the Problems and Methods of Psychoanalysis*. London: Hogarth Press, 1955, pp. 156–67.
31 Michael Balint (1956), *Primary Love and Psycho-analytic Technique*. London: Karnac, 1985. Balint (1967), *The Basic Fault*. London: Routledge, 2013.
32 See for example: *Selected Papers, vol 1* (*Clinical and Theoretical Papers*). Lanham (Maryland): Jason Aronson, 1995.
33 Melanie Klein (1937), "Love, guilt and reparation," in Melanie Klein and Joan Riviere, *Love, Hate and Reparation*. New York: W. W. Norton, 1964, pp. 57–119.
34 Melanie Klein (1957), "Envy and gratitude," in *Envy and Gratitude and Other Works*. London: Random House, 1997, pp. 176–236.
35 Melanie Klein (1947), *Contributions to Psycho-Analysis*. London: Hogarth Press.
36 *Op. cit.*, Klein and Riviere, *Love, Hate and Reparation*, p. 44.
37 *Ibid.*, pp. 87–8.
38 Donald Woods Winnicott (1965), *The Maturational Processes and the Facilitating Environment*. London: Hogarth.
39 Donald Woods Winnicott (1971), *Playing and Reality*. Abingdon: Routledge, 2005, p. 19.
40 *Ibid.*, p. 51.
41 *Ibid.*, p. 188.
42 Donald Woods Winnicott (1952), "Psychosis and childcare," in *Through Pediatrics to Psycho-analysis, Collected Papers*. New York: Brunner-Routledge, 1958, p. 223.
43 *Ibid.*, p. 231
44 Donald Woods Winnicott (2002), "The Development of the Capacity for Concern," in *Winnicott on the Child*. New York: Perseus Publishing Company, Chapter 24, pp. 215–20. Paper presented to the Topeka Psychoanalytic Society, October 12, 1962.
45 "Creativity and its origins," in *op. cit.*, Winnicott, *Playing and Reality*, pp. 87–114.
46 Donald Woods Winnicott (2011), "Communicating and non-communicating, leading to study of certain oppositions," in Lesley Caldwell and Angela Joyce (eds), *Reading Winnicott*. New York, Routledge, p. 192; emphasis in original.
47 Donald Woods Winnicott (1958), "The capacity to be alone," *The International Journal of Psychoanalysis*, vol. 39 (September–October), pp. 416–20.
48 Wilfred Ruprecht Bion (1961), *Experiences in Groups and Other Papers*. London: Tavistock, p. 168. Reprint of Bion (1952), "Group dynamics: A review," *International Journal of Psycho-Analysis*, vol. 33.

38 Some historical points of reference

49 *Ibid.*, pp. 132, 169.
50 *Ibid.*, pp. 134, 169.
51 *Ibid.*, p. 142.
52 *Ibid.*, p. 116.
53 Wilfred Ruprecht Bion (1962), *Learning from Experience*. New York: Basic Books, pp. 28, 31–2, 84–5, 90.
54 *Ibid.*, pp. 35–6.
55 *Ibid.*, p. 91.
56 Henry V. Dicks (1967), *Marital Tensions: Clinical Studies Towards a Psychological Theory of Interaction*. New York: Basic Books.
57 Jürg Willi (1975), *Couples in Collusion: The Unconscious Dimension in Partner Relationships*. New York: Jason Aronson, 1977. Originally published in German as *Zweierbeziehung, Das unbewusste Zusammenspiel von Partnern als Kollusion*. Berlin: Rowohlt Verlag.
58 As of this writing, none of these works have been translated into English (translators' note).
59 Enrique Pichon-Rivière (1965), *El proceso grupal. Del psicoanalisis a la psicologia social*. Buenos Aires: Ediciones Nueva Vision.
60 José Bleger (1967), *Symbiosis and Ambiguity*. East Sussex: Routledge, 2013. Translation of *Simbiosis y ambigüedad: estudio psicoanalitico*. Buenos Aires: Paidos.
61 S. H. Foulkes (1964), *Therapeutic Group Analysis*. London: Karnac, 1984.
62 Jean-Bertrand Pontalis (1963), "Le petit groupe comme objet," in *Après Freud*. Paris: Gallimard, 1993, pp. 257–73.
63 Didier Anzieu (1975), *The Group and the Unconscious*. London: Routledge, 1999. Originally published as *Le groupe et l'inconscient*. Paris: Dunod. The page references are to the original French edition.
64 *Ibid.*, p. 182.
65 René Kaës (2007), *Un singulier pluriel*. Paris: Dunod; Kaës (2009), *Les alliances inconscientes*. Paris: Dunod.
66 *Ibid.*
67 *Ibid.*, p. 192.
68 Jean-Pierre Caillot and Gerard Decherf (1989), *Psychoanalyse du couple et de la famille*. Paris: A. PSY.G.-Editions.
69 Alberto Eiguer (ed.) (1984), *La thérapie psychanalytique du couple*. Paris: Dunod; Eiguer (1998) *La clinique psychanalytique du couple*. Paris: Dunod.
70 *Op. cit.*, Dicks.
71 André Ruffiot (1984), "Le couple et l'amour. De l'originaire au groupe," in Eiguer (ed.), *op. cit.*, *La thérapie psychanalytique du couple*, pp. 85–145.
72 *Op. cit.*, Bion, *Experiences in groups*.
73 *Op. cit.*, Kaës, *Un singulier pluriel*.
74 *Ibid.*
75 André Green (1983), *Life Narcissism, Death Narcissism*. London: Free Association Books, 2001.

Chapter 3

About some fundamental psychic components present within the couple

As the psychic components present and active within the couple are multiple, I have chosen to present some of those psychic components seeming to me to be more specific to this groupal, intersubjective reality in conjunction with the insights of a number of specialists. This will be the case for the sexual component and the "erotic chain," narcissism, affective and instinctual ambivalence, the very obviously mobilized pregenital aspects of each of the partners, the diverse types of conflict, psychic bisexuality, envy and jealousy, Œdipus and sibling complexes, fantasy life, projections and identifications, fusional and symbiotic aspects, transference within the couple and finally the variable modes of object-relations.

The sexual, sexuality and the "erotic chain"

For André Green, "sexuality is defined by the gap between . . . the reproductive function . . . and the search for pleasure which its exercise brings about in its human dimension,"[1] establishing the fundamental difference between biological sexuality and psychosexuality. He considers that it "*is indeed the link uniting sexuality and pleasure which forms the basis of the sexual in psychoanalysis.*"[2] But, the sexual is also characterized by a setting in motion, from excitation to satisfaction.[3]

Moreover, according to him, the major fact of human sexuality is the constancy of the sexual instinctual impulse, which makes it a powerful factor of "imaginative elaboration," to borrow Winnicott's expression,[4] without equivalent within the human psyche.

The pleasure–unpleasure principle would be situated at the center of the "spectrum of sexual phenomena," between, on the one hand, the reality principle appearing as a modified pleasure principle aiming at safeguarding pleasure and guaranteeing protection against certain dangers and, on the other hand, its failure, as in criminal sexuality, especially characterized by the existence of an imperious need, irrepressible pressure, and lack of desire.[5]

Green then suggests conceiving of sexuality from a psychoanalytic perspective as forming an "erotic chain" that would unfurl in a series of formations integrating: instinct and its instinctual impulses; the state of pleasure, and its correlate unpleasure; desire expressed in the form of a state of expectation and of seeking

40 Some fundamental psychic components

fueled by conscious and unconscious representations; fantasies (unconscious or conscious) putting together scenarios for realization of desire; polarization on the Ego or the object, diffraction on love's varieties and derivatives (love for parents, between lovers, friendship, love of humanity, divine love, etc.), enjoyment and finally sublimations.

Green explains that this chain crosses other chains along the way, among them that of the different types of representations and that of the work of the negative, the obvious multiplicity of which justifies calling them "chains of Eros," involving then a double meaning: that of chaining-up the subject and subjecting him or her to his or her eroticism, and that of "chaining" the subject's body to its object and to the aim pursued by sexuality.[6]

Narcissism and its different approaches

I shall now take a look at the different and, nevertheless, very important ideas of Béla Grunberger and André Green.

Béla Grunberger

For Grunberger, the experience that people seek to have repeated is the "prenatal sojourn," out of which they were cast in a traumatizing manner and which they unceasingly desire to recover, a fundamental tendency that he calls the basis of his hypothesis of narcissism.[7]

Grunberger posits the existence of a "state of prenatal elation," source of all the varieties of narcissism. Every subject would retain a definitive imprint of its prenatal sojourn that provides the matrix in which the specific particularities of the narcissism are structured that will later take the form of states and affects, such as the feeling of oneness, self-love, omnipotence, immortality, omniscience, invulnerability, autonomy, etc. However, he observes, all these characteristics are at the same time attributes of the divinity.

After birth, the newborn child undergoes a double trauma. The world of its elation is profoundly perturbed, and it will have to restructure its psychic economy on an objectal, instinctual basis, whence comes the existence of an ongoing conflict between drives and narcissism, as well as of conflictual situations between narcissism (with the narcissistic ideal) and the Ego (and its interests of self-preservation). Living in the illusion of its narcissistic omnipotence, it inevitably runs up against traumatogenic reality leading to the loss of this illusion and to a deep wound. It will have a dual reaction to this: repression and the attempt to recover that omnipotence, or "narcissistic re-establishment" by attributing this to its parents – realizing identity with them through a fusional state or "narcissistic union" – then to idealized, even deified, parental imagos, with all the narcissistic libidinal charge involved in that.

However, this ever alive narcissistic wound will determine varied narcissistic defense reactions. Thus, Grunberger considered all the manifestations of civilization as an array of different human attempts aimed at this narcissistic re-establishment. Analysis would be a narcissistic defense, just as an ideology, a religion or mysticism would be. The "narcissistic union" proceeding from a subject/object confusion, reflecting the fundamental narcissistic union of the fetus with its mother, would be another route to this. He finds it existing between the subject and its alter ego, between patients and their analysts, but also between the two partners of a couple. The latter would also be a narcissistic defense in the spirit of Grunberger.

It seems that the subject's narcissism suffers from the loss of its sexual autonomy, and one of the functions of sexual union would be the restitution of the sensation of narcissistic completeness. Moreover, a successful synthesis of its narcissism and its instinctual Ego is apt to shelter it from feelings of insufficiency.

Human beings are in fact obliged at a very early stage to realize that they are powerless to satisfy themselves in the ways of interest to them and that this powerlessness is their very lot in life, the human condition. Far from accepting this – maintaining the illusion of the omnipotence with which they are born seeming more important than the satisfaction of drives strictly speaking – they set out in search of ways and means of enabling them to reconquer this illusory omnipotence, therefore to maintain this fiction. From then on, the essential thing for them is to succeed in this in one way or another, meaning by re-establishing their narcissistic integrity.

The idea of, and desire for, immortality are connected with moral narcissism, human beings being incapable of admitting that they cannot exist forever and even cannot have always existed: wide-ranging narcissistic compensation for the pitiful brevity of an existence marked by the reality principle.

Grunberger holds that in both the male and the female unconscious, the phallic image expresses narcissistic integrity and completeness in all its forms and that castration, or the partially or totally castrated phallus, represents the difficulties of all kinds that the subject experiences in constituting itself with integrity.

The phallus is a bridge achieving narcissistic completeness as it joins the two members of a couple in coitus.

Each instinctual accomplishment or enrichment of the child's Ego apt to increase its feelings of value, and confirmed as such, will assume a phallic nature in its unconscious, while, inversely, the lack of confirmation, or the unattended to devaluation of narcissistic compensation will be experienced by the child as castration.

This completeness would be realized by the contained/container unit modeled on the intra-utero contained/container fusion realizing the state of feto-maternal completeness.

Finally, Grunberger discusses the presence of guilt linked to narcissism, which he considers the hardest to eliminate. According to him, human beings do not allow themselves to love themselves and to be themselves, and individualism is indisputably looked down upon. Indeed, for him, narcissistic happiness is experienced as a sin, while once it is accepted, it constitutes the essential, obligatory component of the most perfect objectal maturity.[8]

André Green

The concept of One leaves its imprint on the narcissism that Green defines as effacing the trace of the Other within the desire for the One, "unitary utopia."[9] This unity of the Ego as a limited, separate entity denying the divided status of the subject is the culmination of a long history going from absolute primary narcissism to the sexualization of the Ego's drives, work of Eros having at least partially succeeded in the unification of an initially fragmented psyche dominated by the organ pleasure of partial drives.

However, Green points out to us the conflictual situation of the Ego caught between, on the one hand, the compulsion to synthesis, particularly at the origin of narcissism and, on the other, because of its dependence upon the Id, the desire to be but one with the object. When obstacles stand in the way of the realization of this unity of the two in one, solving the identification that realizes the compromise between Ego and object is left to the Ego. The Ego's contradiction is that it wishes to be itself, but can only realize this project through the libidinal contribution of the object with which it wishes to unite itself.

Green considers that primary narcissism cannot be understood as a state, but as a structure. Aspiring to immortal, self-sufficient totality, it evolves in two directions:

- Toward the object-choice. However, secondary narcissism will rob objects of the investments attached to it.
- Toward absolute primary narcissism, where excitation tends toward zero.

In principle, reality and narcissism are at odds with one another, if not mutually self-exclusive. The major contradiction of the Ego is to be the agency that must relate to reality and invest itself narcissistically, while ignoring reality so as only to know itself.

The enemy of narcissism is the reality of the object and, inversely, the object of reality, namely, its function in the economy of the Ego. The object is both external and internal to the Ego, because it is necessary to the foundation of the Ego and to the development of narcissism.

For Green, narcissism serves as a substitute internal object for the subject, which watches over the Ego as a mother watches over her child. *It shelters the subject and overprotects it.*[10]

In addition, Green discusses the conflictuality between narcissism and sexuality, or the disentangling of narcissism from the objectal drives, when he explains that sexuality is at times experienced as competing with narcissism, as if the narcissistic libido risked impoverishing itself by the leakage of object investments; and at other times sexuality only makes sense so far as it feeds the subject's narcissism. Sexual enjoyment becomes evidence of preserved narcissistic integrity.[11]

Aggressiveness is the object of the same disentanglement. There is a lot of talk about the need for narcissistic domination. There are objectal satisfactions that are linked to the position of mastery, and the impossibility of quenching the need for mastery leads to narcissistic rage.

The ultimate goal of narcissism is to abolish the primary difference, that of the One and the Other, leading to the abolition of all the other differences, as well as sexual differences.

Instinctual and affective ambivalence

Eros/instinct of destruction

The love-object is always "bi-instinctually" invested (Eros links the death drive), which provides an instinctual basis for the fundamental affective ambivalence (love/hate) of the relationship. It is also entangling, and therefore protects from any danger of instinctual disunion by the very fact of this entanglement.

According to Benno Rosenberg (1991), this instinctual antagonism produces a conflict in the Ego/object relationship which has multiple repercussions. Thus, in order to constitute the unity of the object, for its "internal bond-cohesiveness," Eros must succeed in constituting it and preserving it, just as the death drive must not succeed in disintegrating it. But, it is also necessary that, as an effect of a well-tempered disentanglement, the destruction instinct can establish internal differentiations within the object contributing to both the complexity of its structuring and to its richness, something which will permit the Ego to establish a varied, nuanced objectal relationship. Finally, he considers that a good relationship between Eros and its object, between desire and its object, necessarily involves the participation of the destruction instinct that places them at a tolerable distance from one another, thus making development of the desire possible while avoiding direct collusion between the desiring Ego and its object.[12]

Love/hate

For Freud in *Instincts and Their Vicissitudes* (1915),[13] the story of the appearance of love and its objectal relations brings us to understand why it so often seems ambivalent, that is to say, accompanied by hatred directed toward the same object. After an initial narcissistic, auto-erotic stage, the oral stage leads to the desire to incorporate or devour the object that is compatible with the elimination of the object's individuality and displays clear ambivalence.

Then, in the anal stage, there is a push toward gaining ascendancy and possession of the object associated with hatred, but without destruction. At the genital stage, love is at odds with hate. Thus, this hate mixed with love partly comes from the preliminary stages of love.

Some pregenital aspects

The oral, anal and urethro-phallic components are active and coordinate between the partners in diverse ways, both in their sexual life and in the types and levels of pregenital object-relations that they construct and mobilize in their couple.

44 Some fundamental psychic components

But let us rather look at the masochism that seems to me to play a major role as other, different, "guardian" of the durability of couple – alongside the inhibiting of the drive's aim, narcissistic investment and the sublimated homosexual impulses – through its distinct contribution to sustaining the relationship and making it last with all its vicissitudes.

It is to Benno Rosenberg (1991) that we owe this insight of prime importance. He has in fact reminded us that there exists in each one of us a primary erogenous masochistic kernel, the first form of drive entanglement (Eros, force of binding that binds the death drive, force of unbinding), constitutive of the Ego's primary kernel, conditioning its existence with the presence of primary narcissism. According to him, masochism is involved in every object-relation and makes it possible, which means that it permits the investment of excitation and inevitable tensions involved in excitation by making them bearable. It makes possible the unsatisfying relationship, immediate non-discharge, the postponement of satisfaction, therefore, making expectation possible and participating in this way in the instinctual dimension of the reality principle.

Consequently, *masochism confers upon every subject the capacity to make a love relationship last over time.* Evaluating the significance of the primary erogenous masochistic kernel at the heart of this relationship would prove essential. He further considers that masochism precedes sadism, just as drive entanglement precedes projection. What is then projected outside and becomes sadism is masochism, sadism therefore becoming a projected masochism, a masochism experienced projectively via the object. It would then be a matter of necessary defense in relation to primary masochism which, without that, would take up all the room by itself, would isolate the Ego from the object and become deadly.[14]

I shall point to the presence of the exhibitionism/voyeurism pair also active in varying doses and modalities.

Concerning some major conflicts

Multiple drive investments, a varied interplay of identifications and projections flow through every couple. But, every couple is also animated by structural and conjunctural conflicts –major ones in the case of certain of them – organizing the conjugal dynamic. Thus, at work are the dynamic antagonisms between: identity/alterity, Ego/object, Eros/destructive drives, self-preservation/sexuality, narcissism/objectality, pregenitality/genitality, male/female, bisexuality/sexual identity, especially.

Since certain of these antagonisms have already been considered, or will be later on, I shall discuss the major identity/alterity and male/female conflicts prevailing within the intersubjective relationship.

The identity/alterity conflict

This reflects the first, primordial difference between the Ego and the non-Ego, that between the "One" and the "Other." This irreducible, narcissistically unacceptable difference co-organizes the structural conflictuality of the intersubjective dimension of all couples. Green thinks that pain is involved in the recognition of alterity, but also that a wound is involved in not being able to be the Other. If the ultimate aim of each of the partners' narcissism is the abolition, the effacing of this primordial difference experienced in the fusional state of "narcissistic union," identification would, according to Green, be the response of "negativity" to alterity.

Jean Cournut (2001) considers that if this primordial difference is disturbing because it separates, it is constructive precisely because this separating makes it possible to open up the space necessary for thinking and self-representation. He explains that, without alterity, one cannot represent oneself, recognize oneself or identify oneself, but there is a price to pay for the necessary alterity, and the price is that of difference and of everything it entails in terms of distress, because the difference is sexual first of all, something which again accentuates what is irrepresentable, unthinkable about the other person. It is this matter of the unthinkable, of the irrepresentable, the unknown that human beings run up against.[15]

The male/female conflict

The psychosexual male/female dichotomy is constituted during puberty, coming thus after the active/passive dichotomy of the anal phase and the phallic/castrated dichotomy of the phallic phase. Unlike the latter, this dichotomy points to a genuine difference, that of the difference between the sexes, object of a conflict – intrapsychic as much as it is intersubjective – which will represent one of the major conflicts in the life of any couple.

Cournut suggests prior differentiation of the male/female dichotomy – designating categories of humanness, the characteristics of which are found in both sexes – from the dichotomy contrasting masculinity/femininity, implying a set of qualities with which both men and women are endowed.

He differentiates between the representable, castrated female arousing castration anxiety and the irrepresentable – therefore anxiety-provoking – orgasmic female. Furthermore, the female is erotico-maternal in both men and women.

I have chosen to orient my exploration of this male/female conflict by taking particular interest in the fear that the various different aspects of the female arouses in men, something which contributes to making this conflict more complex. Endeavoring to respond to this, Cournut thinks that they do not succeed in seeing the female defined as an erotico-maternal whole.

He explains that to the extent that men believe – still according to Freud – that women incarnate the "castrated female," they awaken men's fear of castration. To avert that fear, they adorn women with qualities, jewelry, fetishes, with maternity also, and extol femininity erected in all its phallic splendor ("she has everything for herself, lacks nothing"). The other way of averting the fear consists of using women's sexuality for the greater pleasure of both parties.[16]

But the female is also what is irrepresentable about the woman's orgasmic erotic body and about the maternal womb, as well as the always possible, unbearable

46 Some fundamental psychic components

disappearance of this omnipotent mother figure. This disappearance would in fact constitute an irrepresentable, never really elaborated, ever present, initial trauma. It would be included in the erotico-maternal female and be at the origin of a "melancholic nucleus," Cournut explains. In this way, men would be protected against the melancholic consequences of this loss by the nature of the castration complex, which functions as an ongoing, structuring phobia, trading the part for the whole. What is irrepresentable in women, their "female," would be, he considers, the possibility of being abandoned pointlessly, for no reason, without anything. He is indicating there one of the essential components of the difference between the sexes whose major repercussions on conjugal functioning, in critical, conflictual periods especially, have too often been underestimated.

Psychic bisexuality

The psychic bisexuality of each of the partners is also mobilized within every couple. It very obviously does not correspond to the fantasy of bisexuality – being and having both sexes – a universal megalomaniacal fantasy denying the difference between the sexes and alterity, with denial of separation. We must give this up and accept a unisexual fate!

Psychic bisexuality is an outcome of male and female identifications. Nevertheless, the female in men will be different from that of women, just as the male in women will be different from that of men.

In men, a distinction is made between the primary female linked to the primary identification with the maternal female – even the "pure female" resulting from a primary identification with the breast – and the female brought into play in the negative Œdipus complex, while women's introjective identification with the maternal female is followed by an identification with the genital femaleness of their mothers. Men's bisexuality is also different from that of women. How do they interconnect in heterosexual couples?

Underlying the complete Œdipus complex, psychic bisexuality obliges one to consider the love relation, at least, as a union having four components (the male and the female in each partner), where each component must find a form of satisfaction – be it direct, or indirect – fantasized, symbolic, or sublimated. The homosexual component as the basis of friendly relations (through sublimation and inhibition of the aim of instincts) plays, according to Lemaire, a very great role in this very special friendship, a component so necessary for all conjugal life owing to the tender attachment it communicates. Being one of the products of the negative Œdipus complex of each of the partners, it facilitates the narcissistic object-choice and is a factor in the durability of the couple. When it is not sufficiently "utilized" in the functioning of the couple, the conjugal relationship finds itself impoverished by this, and each of the partners may look for a satisfactory object outside the couple.

In his key work on psychic bisexuality, Christian David (1992)[17] has explored the full extent and complexity of this concept. Bisexuality constitutes a major

Some fundamental psychic components   47

experience of psychosexuality, and the very processes of *psychosexualization* and *psycho-bisexualization* themselves give birth to sexuality as human sexuality.

He suggests that, in parallel and inverse relation to the differentiating, evolving process through which sexual identity asserts itself – along with what that involves in terms of narcissistic reassurance and exacerbation of the feeling of incompleteness – a bisexualizing process exists that would tend toward the internalization of psycho-sexual difference in the form of an accentuation of the complementary schemes of the other sex present within each one's psyche as potentiality more or less suscepti-ble to being aroused or awakened. This presence does not, moreover, appear as the work of innateness as much as it does the work of original intersubjectivity.[18]

And it is the fact that the gendered individual him- or herself bears the comple-mentarity of the other sex in a virtual form that would make the sexual relationship possible. David maintains that a sexual relationship *exists*, a relationship *exists* between the sexes, because there is bisexuality. There is bisexuality, because there is incompleteness in each of the sexes, felt by each one in his or her way as castra-tion. Neither of the two sexes can pride itself on possessing the phallus.[19] Psychic bisexuality is thus potentiality playing a role of mediator (bisexual mediation), both in the psychosexual and sexual intersubjective exchanges and in the inter- and intra-systemic relations within each of us. If the complementarity that it represents increases excessively at the expense of the specific sexuality or psychosexuality connected with the actual sex, it could also represent an obstacle to the flow of fantasies and investments.

He further emphasizes that the economy of each one's sexuality rests on an ever unstable relationship between asserting bisexuality and asserting sexual specificity. Finally, he considers that if the integration of psychic bisexuality is achieved satisfactorily, one will find that the sexuality acted upon and lived out almost never leads to bisexual behavior, but succeeds in channeling the male and female impulses within a heterosexual relationship.

Envy and jealousy

The reciprocal movements associated with envy need to be looked at in connec-tion with Melanie Klein's invaluable contributions presented earlier and, in my opinion, be principally seen within the context of the two partners' sibling com-plexes as reactivated by conjugal life in the same way as jealousy is.

Jealousy, according to Freud

Freud considered jealousy to be a normal affective state, like mourning. He dis-cerned three different forms of it: competitive or normal, projected, and delusional:[20]

- *Normal jealousy* is part of love life and is characterized by the pain caused by the love-object that one believes one has lost, combined with narcissistic humiliation, self-criticism on the part of the Ego itself and hostility toward the rival in question. It reactivates the complete Œdipus complex, the sibling complex, and is experienced *bisexually* by many people. In a man, there is pain caused by the woman loved and hatred for the male rival, but it may also have the effect of strengthening the mourning of the man unconsciously loved and hatred for the female rival (reactivation of the negative Œdipus).

- In *projected jealousy*, there are unconscious fantasies of infidelity, and the denial of one's own temptations leads to projecting one's impulses on the other person.
- *Delusional jealousy* falls into the category of delusional psychosis.

The Œdipus and sibling complexes

The Œdipus and sibling complexes (archaic and oedipal forms)[21] are major psychic organizers of couples and their interplay between the two partners needs to be explored.

Besides the role of oedipal organization in the triangular structuring of the life of every subject, which distributes its heterosexual and homosexual investments between its couple and the "world of others" – that is to say, its social universe in the broad sense – in a later chapter, I shall discuss the impact of the Œdipus complex on the love choice and the modes of structuring conjugal life, as well as looking at the often underestimated role of the sibling complex in the choice of partners and in conjugal life.

Fantasy life

Appealing to Bion's ideas, then to Anzieu's, one could conceive of the couple, just as any group, as functioning on two levels, that of fantasizing activity and that of "work group," or "technical pole." In keeping with contemporary French conceptions, to which I partially subscribe, I consider that the couple's fantasy dimension comes into play at diverse levels. First of all, the individual fantasies of one party harmonizing with those of the partner, as well as their primal fantasies, will play the role of organizers of the couple. In addition, conscious conjugal flow of fantasies in the form of common, shared reveries, fruitful, but also unconscious "interfantasizing" – having both stimulating and paralyzing effects – will be at work and will nourish the couple, as well as contributing to structuring it. It will especially produce *compromise conjugal formations* (myths, ideologies and other expressions of conjugal culture) belonging to this groupal reality – common, shared psychic reality – and a fantasy of the couple, or couple-object, in each of them, a psychic object above all invested narcissistically and a unified representation of the couple endowed with an imaginary common body and common psyche, according to Caillot and Decherf. Finally, let us recall, in keeping with Anzieu's ideas, that as any group, the couple fantasizes itself as being a living body of which each one recognizes him- or herself as a member and where oral fantasizing is prevalent. Anzieu wrote that the group is a mouth. This fantasy of a body proper to the group would then be a response to the nostalgic dream of a symbiotic union between the members of the group in a primitive maternal womb. I shall expand upon this most pertinent conception.

Projections and identifications

Projections and introjective, projective, adhesive, primary identifications contribute to structuring couples, producing a localized effacing of the psychic boundaries of the two partners, henceforth interpenetrated. Nevertheless, it would be appropriate also to specify their diverse effects, both within each partner's Ego and upon the intersubjective relationship. Kaës emphasizes that in their diverse modes, they constitute processes at the basis of phenomena of fantasized resonance and of interfantasizing. In addition, they partake in the organization of the "apparatus of the psyches" of the couple's partners, constituting together a specifically conjugal psychic reality. Let us also remember their defensive function vis-à-vis the object that has become internalized, but also in the service of the Ego. I now propose to clarify certain of these aspects.

As concerns projection, Green considers that, in the love relationship, each partner is but a prop liable to receive the projected representation of the other partner. Even if each one has him- or herself represented by his or her projections, the problem would become one of the relationship of two projective activities.

The field of identifications is vast. As a primary expression of an affective bond with another person, and ambivalent from the start (being an outgrowth of the oral stage), the forcefulness of incorporation fantasies there underlies identification, and it must be distinguished, on the one hand, from introjection – the fantasized passing of an object, of its qualities, to within the Ego without modifying it – and, on the other hand, from internalization, which concerns intersubjective relationships, conflicts, which have then been transformed into intrapsychic relationships.

It seems important to me to remind readers right away of some essential functions and characteristics of identifications that will help us better understand their impact on the construction of the couple. I shall do this in conjunction with the invaluable contribution made by Pierre Luquet and his remarkable work *Les identifications* (2003).[22]

Luquet first of all reminds us of the Ego's narcissistic need to expand, the initial narcissistic trauma tied to the need for the object and to its dependency, introjection, as an essential defense against the absence of the real object, against the loss of the structuring object, as well as the notion of investment of boundaries, of limits by every subject's Ego. It can then broaden by including a greater portion of the outside world.

He considers identification to be an objectal relationship in which subject and object are joined by libidinal investments. He establishes an initial distinction between the identification that occurs in the total Ego, or *total identification* – corresponding to the "assimilation" of the object, which thus becomes a constituent of the Ego, something which therefore presupposes fusion with it and taking charge

50 Some fundamental psychic components

of its function by the Ego – and that occurring within a limited zone of the boundary of the Ego, the extension of which forms an "imago" or "inclusion." Luquet furthermore tells us that introjection does not always result in identification, since the objects can remain internal without there really being any modification of the Ego.

Luquet differenciates – in accordance with the evolution of the Ego, the libidinal organization, the objectal relations – narcissistic identifications (such as projective identification), which are massive and particularly active in structuring the couple, from late identifications (hysterical ones, in particular), which are partial, limited and constitute a complex phenomenon implying, among other things: a clear, externalized representation of the object of identification; its fragmentation into diverse aspects, one of which is an optional choice; selective introjection, due to the structuring of anality; counter-identification with respect other elements of the real object.

Among the diverse functions of identification, he has identified:

- The protection of the Ego and of the object, therefore, identification's defensive role within the organization of the Ego. Thus, within what is assimilated to the Ego, the inhibitory function of instinctual restraint of the Ego would be essential, because instinctual discharge places the Ego and the object in danger. Within the objectal relationship, the Ego will find the investment of possibilities of inhibition of its desires by assimilation of prohibiting objects which, felt to be protective, will allow the instinctual inhibition.
- Its participation in gratification and preserving it from lack of gratification.
- Its opposition to aggression against the person with whom one identifies.
- Its role in knowing and recognizing the feelings of others.

The fusional and symbiotic aspects

These would correspond to the regressive desire to return to the fetal state, therefore, to the mother's womb, as well as to the "mother–infant unit" described by Winnicott. From the perspective of Grunberger's thought, this pursuit of "narcissistic union" with the partner aims at the "re-establishment of that narcissistic integrity," which each of us lost too early, and produces a state of "narcissistic completeness" expressed by the phallic image in the unconscious of each partner. From the Winnicottian perspective, this state of regained unity corresponding to primary narcissism would also correspond to the "pure female" experience of being that is based on that of omnipotence, enabling the establishment of a feeling of Self, a non-instinctual subject/object identity situated at the opposite pole of the "pure male" characterized by the instinctual objectal relation. We could in fact also envisage such organization within the couple around two separate poles: one narcissistic and groupal, non-conflictual, site of omnipotent massive narcissistic investments, "pure female," based on the Ego/love-object identity, conferring a feeling of "conjugal self"; the other, objectal, intersubjective, conflictual, site of aggressive, erotic, narcissistic investments, "pure male," based on the objectal instinctual Ego/love-object relation.

Some fundamental psychic components 51

Constituting a "conjugal total Self," this bipolar organization would consequently express the "couple's bisexuality."

These fusional, symbiotic aspects have erogenous value, but also generate depersonalization anxieties, something which creates fairly ongoing oscillation between the desire for fusion (groupal, narcissistic pole) and the necessary protective distancing (intersubjective, objectal pole) within the couple. Taking a look at Rosenberg's ideas, we find that the relative dosages of Eros and death drive will therefore necessarily be variable. At the narcissistic pole, Eros would be predominant, but potentially destructive of the Ego's boundaries, while at the objectal pole, the antagonistic relationship between Eros and the instinct of destruction structures the intersubjective relationship and protects the boundaries of the Ego.

Transference within the couple

Already detected by Freud in *Observations on Transference-Love* (1915), transference is powerfully at work within the psychic life of couples all throughout their existence, coming into play in the love choice and compelling the partners to replay infantile fantasy scenarios in particular. Within the couple, one in fact encounters a twofold repetition: that of the state of being in love that consists of "new editions of old traits" that repeats "infantile reactions," "the essential character of every state of being in love," according to Freud.[23] However, transference fits into a transferential and inter-transferential relationship between the two partners, whence comes the second repetition represented by the transference, which "is itself only a piece of repetition, and that the repetition is a transference of the forgotten past not only on to the doctor but also on to all other aspects of the current situation."[24] It fell to Freud to discuss the artificial creation of a *transference neurosis* that would be "treated" by analytic work.

I have also observed in couples a form of *inter-transferential neurosis*, within which, through his or her actions, each partner repeats "infantile reactions" with his or her current love partner. Nevertheless, unlike transference onto the psychoanalyst, this is a matter of inter-transference between the two conjugal partners left to their own devices in a double relationship without any possible formulation and, even less, any therapeutic work with the help of a couple therapist. The couple will consequently find themselves locked into the *inter-transferential neurosis* they created together.

Object-relations

Several aspects of object-relations need to be taken into consideration and explained. What objects are we talking about: external or internal objects; real or fantasized objects; partial objects or total objects; "good" or "bad" objects; narcissistic objects or erotic objects? What types of prevalent relation and instinctual investment are at work: real or fantasized object-relations; total object-relation or partial object-relation; pregenital object-relation or genital object-relation;

52 Some fundamental psychic components

narcissistic relation or objectal relation; aim-inhibited, sublimated, homosexual, heterosexual, aggressive, erotic, narcissistic investments? Within the couple's organization and functioning, we shall find multiple and diverse modes of object-relations – stable, because structuring, in the case of some of them, and variable for others – inherent in certain circumstances of the psychic life of each partner, as well as in the vicissitudes of conjugal life.

The light shed on this by Maurice Bouvet's ideas has proven particularly helpful to me, as have Grunberger's ideas on oral and anal object-relations. I shall finally present certain of Green's ideas about the structural, primal Ego/object conflict.

Maurice Bouvet[25]

Thinking along the lines of Freud's and Karl Abraham's viewpoints, but also influenced by Melanie Klein's and Paul Federn's ideas, Bouvet has stressed the importance of exploring the field of object-relations as a basis for a psychoanalytical clinical approach.

First of all, he discusses the existence of interrelationships among the Ego, the "drive-equilibrium," and the object-relations, which he defines as systems of the subject's relationships with its internal and external "significant" objects. Then, he goes on to differentiate between two principal types of them, pregenital and genital, in terms of a certain number of notions, namely those of: fixation; regression; projection; introjection; fantasized activity; tools of the object-relation; "objectal distance" – with "drawing near" and "stretching," its mechanisms of accommodation and of "adjustment" especially, consisting of defensive procedures guarding against the danger of the appearance of depersonalization. He also discusses the existence of variations of relational levels and of the Ego's structure in one and the same subject, which is particularly illuminating for the couple.

Moreover, he considers that the object-relation is both an objectal relation and a narcissistic relation in the sense that narcissistic organization is necessarily accomplished via the subject's relations with an object. The object-relation therefore receives a double drive investment.

The genital object-relation indicates normality, and certain neurotic organizations centered on the œdipal conflict lead to an object-relation taking into account the object's reality, the total object perceived in its alterity, while the pregenital object-relation refers to pregenital stages of fixation, such as the oral and anal stages. It is characterized by the possessive, captative nature of the relationship and the subject's need for this relationship, later expanded upon using the expression "anaclitic object-relation," that is to say, the narcissistic need to lean on an object that can play, according to Bouvet, the role of "auxiliary Ego." He observes that it is peculiar to the pregenital object-relation that it possesses the characteristic of being both absolute necessity and stifling constraint. Due to the fixation of a major part of the personality on an earlier pregenital stage, the complete, normal genital relationship, love, is by essence rapprochement in the course of which the subject gives up the boundary lines of his or her personality to merge

Some fundamental psychic components   53

for a moment with the other person. However, in pregenital personalities, love is really a form of destruction, a threat to the subject's integrity. This is the dilemma characteristic of pregenital object-relations.

For his part, *Grunberger* enquires into oral and anal object-relations – pregenital object-relations, according to Bouvet – and prior to that discusses the existence of pregenitality having a dialectic dynamic, that of the opposition between orality and anality.

According to him, one must consider orality as having its roots in narcissism, meaning in prenatal life, and its existence as "straddling" pre- and postnatal life. It would be a matter of a pre-ambivalent, "anobjectal" phase, and the ambivalent phase would be connected with the infiltration of sadistic elements of the anal-sadistic phase.

The oral object-relation would be characterized by subject/object confusion, the oral forming a genuine unit with its complement. It would be blurred, imprecise, but absolute and unlimited. The oral, therefore, knows nothing of the object as such, nor of its own nature as an object, its Ego, and therefore its limits. Its world is an open world, and its relational mode is above all governed by this trait. Giving and receiving are equivalent as long as everything takes place within the fusion. It recognizes neither the principle of exchange, nor scales of values. It desires total, immediate gratification. Although experienced very intensely – but on the affective, rather than on the sexual plane itself – oral love life is always superficial from the point of view of drive maturation.

What about the anal object-relation?

Grunberger holds that this type of relationship must rather take as its point of departure the retention factor, basis of anal mastery and motilty, and he detects the existence of an anal component within each objectal relation component which is at the latter's energy base. This fact would be made obligatory by the distant origin of the object constituted as such, the excremental object, both narcissistic and objectal, a manipulable object, source of pleasure and mastery.

He points out to us that the essential characteristic of this anal relation would lie in objectal mastery, costing the subject the restoration of his or her narcissistic integrity. The anal positions itself opposite, and above, its object, whose subjectness is denied, and it creates a distance which delimits it in relation to it. The object's own quality or essence are of little significance since the objects only serve as props for certain functions and, therefore, are interchangeable. This anal object-relation is a typical subject/object relationship, a social relationship *par excellence*, unlike the oral relation, the basis of all future discrimination, scale of values, organization and hierarchization. All constructive forms of human activity therefore depend on anality.

Appealing to these insights, we could conceive of the necessary synergetic and antagonic participation of oral and anal components, in varied doses, in any construction of a couple, the oral object-relation being particularly mobilized at the "group" level, that of the couple's fantasy – unified representation of an imaginary common body and common psyche – while the anal object-relation prevails

54 Some fundamental psychic components

on the conflictual, intersubjective level, organizing conjugal life and *work couple*. I shall expand upon this reflection at a later point.

Green and the Ego/object conflict, exemplary of the clinical study of borderline states

First of all, according to Green, the object-relation includes the object-representation and corresponding affects, as well as the Ego's affects without Ego-representation. The representations of the Ego would in fact be object-representations that disguise themselves as Ego-representations through narcissistic investment.

The Ego would associate the functioning of a network of operations (perception, representation, identification) with a system of investments of a relatively constant level that the lack of object could disturb. The object, which is, however, originally the goal of the Id's gratifications, is actually in certain respects always a cause of unbalance for the Ego, a *trauma*, whence comes the expression *trauma-object*. Indeed, the Ego would be torn between two contradictory tendencies: that aspiring to unitary unification that extends to unification with the object, with the danger of becoming disorganized; and that separating it from the object upon which it is dependent, an intolerable situation, and also disorganizing. From that point on, the problem of the relations between Ego and object would, therefore, be that of their coexistence and their limits, internal as well as external, limits in tune with those between Id and Ego. The object, therefore, represents a threat to the Ego in that, just by existing, it forces the Ego to modify its own system of functioning, and by its uncontrollability is a source of traumas, because the object, upon which the Ego is painfully dependent, is changing, unknowable, unpredictable. It is autonomous and not comparable to a narcissistic object. Consequently, accepting the object is accepting its variability, its vicissitudes, that is to say that it may penetrate the Ego and leave it, thus reviving anxieties of intrusion and separation. This is why the conflict between the Ego and the trauma-object proves inevitable.

Notes

1 André Green (1997), *The Chains of Eros, The Sexual in Psychoanalysis*. London: Karnac, 2008, p. 30. Translation of *Les chaînes d'Eros, l'actualité du sexuel*. Paris: Odile Jacob, 1997, p. 271.
2 *Ibid.*, p. 214, of the French edition. Green's emphasis.
3 *Ibid.*, p. 211.
4 For example, Winnicott, *op. cit.*, *Playing and Reality*, p. 3.
5 *Op. cit.*, Green, p. 214, of the French edition.
6 *Ibid.*, pp. 123, 211. Also, André Green (1993). *Le travail du négatif*. Paris: Minuit. English translation: *The Work of the Negative*, translated by Andrew Weller. London: Free Association Books, 1999.
7 Béla Grunberger (1971). *Le narcissisme*. Paris: Payot & Rivages, 1971. p. 25. English translation: *Narcissism: Psychoanalytic Essays*. Madison, CT: International Universities Press, 1979.
8 *Ibid.*, p. 235 of the French edition.

Some fundamental psychic components 55

9 André Green (1983). *Life Narcissism, Death Narcissism.* London: Free Association Books, 2001, p. 25. Translation of *Narcissisme de vie, narcissisme de mort.* Paris: Les Editions de Minuit, 1983, p. 24.

10 *Ibid.*, p. 51 of the French edition.

11 *Ibid.*, p. 42 of the French edition.

12 *Op. cit.*, Rosenberg, pp. 127–8.

13 *Op. cit.*, Freud, *Instincts and Their Vicissitudes.*

14 *Op. cit.*, Rosenberg.

15 Jean Cournut (2001). *Pourquoi les hommes ont peur des femmes.* Paris: Presses universitaires de France, 2006. p. 51.

16 *Ibid.*, pp. 210–11.

17 Christian David (1992). *La biisexualité psychique.* Paris: Payot & Rivages, 1997.

18 *Ibid.*, p. 50.

19 *Ibid.*, p. 59.

20 Sigmund Freud (1922), *Some Neurotic Mechanisms in Jealousy, Paranoia and Homosexuality. S.E.*, 18, London: Hogarth.

21 René Kaës (2008). *Le complexe fraternel.* Paris: Dunod.

22 Pierre Luquet (2003). *Les identifications.* Paris: Presses universitaires de France.

23 *Op. cit.*, Freud, *Observations on Transference-Love*, p. 168.

24 Sigmund Freud (1914b), *Remembering, Repeating and Working-Through. S.E.*, 12, London: Hogarth, p. 151.

25 Maurice Bouvet (1960). *La relation d'objet.* Paris: Presses universitaires de France, 2006. p. 139.

Chapter 4

Sketching a "natural" history of the couple

As the history of every couple is vast and complex, I have most particularly chosen to discuss certain of its potentially critical, mutative and structuring stages by combining several complementary approaches, therefore conferring upon it a much greater degree of intelligibility. These stages are: the meeting, the conditions of choice of partner and modalities of structuring the couple; the first stages of life as a couple, followed by potentially critical times making it possible to think through the psychic processes of crisis and its prospects for evolution; the development of a conjugal culture and identity by paying particular attention to certain areas (the domestic realm and distribution of roles, communication and communications, conflicts, conjugal rhythms and, finally, sexual life); the matter of desiring a child; the birth of a child, or the critical, mutative transition from the couple to the family and its impact on the couple's psychic economy and dynamic and on each of its members; the couple that is childless by choice or owing to sterility, its causes and repercussions. Other than the possible enlargement of the family – its stages marked by the life cycles of the children and the diverse events experienced by its members inevitably having destabilizing impact on the conjugal and family dynamic and economy – I shall look at the disruptive period of the couple's aging, its characteristics, its effects, what is at stake in it.

The meeting, choice of partner and the couple's modalities of psychic structuring

Sociological approach to meeting and choosing a partner

Major studies in France (Girard, 1964; Bozon and Héran, 1987) have highlighted an important social mechanism determining and limiting the choice of partners and operatives in preserving and reproducing the social order: the phenomenon of homogamy with its different geographic, professional, cultural components.[1] *Nobody at all marries just anybody at all, and birds of a feather stick together.* This finding runs counter to presently prevailing perceptions according to which

Sketching a "natural" history of the couple 57

couples are based on love and chance meeting. Nevertheless, this search for a future partner similar to oneself is not systematic and it may be just as important to look for differences, fitting in then with "social rules of correspondence" difficult to disassociate from "the interplay of social actors." They vary historically in connection with the changes in tastes and mores, with the evolution of relationships between social groups. The search for complementarity, therefore, for differences that are diverse in nature, will be a source of richness specific to each party and made up of what we are the least endowed with. Coordinating the resemblances/differences, central in the formation of the couple, is a complex, dynamic process. Consequently, sociologists are asking themselves why, since marriage markets are becoming more open, public opinion is growing more favorable to heterogamy, homogamy is remaining quasi-stable, declining very slowly? Why is free love not upsetting the system of social connections?[2] These questions have led the author to take an interest in the manner in which the choice is concretely made.

A first group of explanations refers back to the concrete conditions of the couple's meeting and the beginnings of forming the couple. Michel Bozon and François Héran[3] have analyzed the meeting places, which are socially constructed in such a way that nobody at all meets just anybody at all. These specialists trace a "triangle of meetings" existing between "public places," "reserved places" and "private places." Each socio-professional category would then be positioned in relation to these three poles. Thus, common people would meet in public places (at celebrations, fairs, dances, in the street, cafés, shopping centers), the upper classes with intellectual baggage in places reserved for them, access to which is symbolically or materially controlled (associations, places of study, clubs, cultural activities, sports), professionals of the private sector, bosses, liberal professions in private places (homes, family celebrations, among friends). Frequentation of these specific places therefore determines the people who frequent them.

The second group of explanations involves the categories in terms of which the partner is chosen. Bozon has highlighted the existence of social criteria based on the internalization of "categories of perception" that differ in terms of the milieu of origin and a person's gender. He thus shows how physical criteria and the evaluation of moral and psychological qualities establish connections between the candidates of both sexes.

Kaufmann has hypothesized that, while fleeting unions are becoming more open, more heterogamous, by verifying the two partners' ability to get along with one another, the early stages of life together later act as a filter. A portion of the most atypical unions disappears, while the most homogamous ones (or most complementary ones) more readily remain stable. Paradoxically, free love and conjugal instability do not, therefore, keep homogamy from being perpetuated. The dynamic vision is essential here, because it is not a matter of simple continuity. The process leading to this outcome is very different from what it was in the past. It is based much more on the actors' capacity for action and decision.[4]

58 Sketching a "natural" history of the couple

A psychoanalytical approach to the meeting, the choice of partner and the modalities of structuring the couple

The meeting

The romantic meeting causes a trauma, a breaking into the partners' psyches, which produces an upheaval of greater or lesser significance on the economic, dynamic and topographical levels. Jacques André considers that a profound kinship with femininity is perceptible through this aspect of breaking in, in which each person's Ego is attacked and dispossessed, which would, then, be the *quality of romantic openness to alterity*.[5]

The meeting, then the love relationship and structuring of the couple would indeed be analogous in some respects to the conditions inaugurating the psychogenesis of femininity as Jacques André has defined them. This traumatic, invasive dimension of the meeting and of the mutual intrapsychic penetration of the seductive and seducing object, combined with a movement of openness and drive passivation, not only update this primal situation of "primitive femininity," but also make it one of the primordial conditions without which there could not be any romantic meeting, much less a couple. There is, in fact, a coordinating of a dual – intersubjective and intrapsychic – movement at work in each one of the partners that combines with that of the other. This situation would therefore mobilize the femininity of each one of the partners, as well as his or her masculine–penetrating and "instinctually-invasive" component. Finally, as Christian David has maintained, it is the psychic bisexuality of the two partners that makes their romantic encounter possible.[6]

The choice of object

The romantic object must be at the origin of narcissistic, erotic, tender and aggressive forms of satisfaction, and at the same time contribute to strengthening the Ego and its defensive organization, especially in those areas in which it is rather weak in face of a never entirely controllable balance of drives.[7] It must in this way procure a state of psychic security that is never definitively acquired.[8]

Each partner's Œdipus is going to predetermine this choice of object, which will in fact be made in two phases of what is called the diphasic evolution of sexuality (infantile sexuality, latent phase, then puberty). In the course of this evolution, there will be a converging of two currents – tender and sensual – in the same object and a joining of pregenital partial drives, with genitality having primacy, effectively leading to genital love and to the genital aim.

Using some remarkable work by Lemaire, allow me to present some types of choice of object:

- Choice in reference to the parental *imagos*, that is to say œdipal choices. These references are positive, but may be negative with regard to a parent of the opposite sex, but also of the same sex. The role of psychic bisexuality and male and female identifications is particularly patent.
- Choice of object and pregenital drives.

The romantic object is used as a means of protection against the diverse expressions of partial drives isolated from the whole and having to be kept repressed and counter-invested. It is therefore a matter of a defensive choice.

- Choice in reference to the positive and negative imagos of the parental couple, referring to the fantasy of the primal scene as source of inspiration and creation, but also within a defensive perspective.
- Choice of narcissistic object.
  What one is oneself, what one oneself was, what one oneself would like to be (the Ego's Ideal) and the person who was a part of one's own self.
- Choice of defect.
  Narcissistic advantages can also be obtained from the choice of negative characteristics in the partner. There, it is the object's latent weakness that is chosen on the very level upon which the subject itself fears being weak. It would be a matter of attributing to the partner the weakness one fears in oneself. This choice would contribute to determining a systemic organization of the couple with an unconscious distribution of roles.
- The partner as a prop for bad, internalized objects.
  Generally, in an initial phase, the partner is an object of desire and invested as good, but very ambivalently so, something which will be reversed secondarily. The object becoming a source of frustration and persecution, the dual investment − narcissistic and erotic − must at least endure longer than the aggressive investment. It will, nevertheless, remain "objectalized," invested as a "bad object" that preserves a value for the two partners. Indeed, certain subjects, habitually disturbed by significant difficulties in their relationships behave as if they needed a partner to hate, without which they sink into greater troubles, such as persecution delirium. There we could identify, for example, a sadomasochistic game between an object identified with a masochistic Ego and a subject identified with a sadistic Superego.
- The choice of the partner as protection against the risk of intense love and to keep from being swallowed up or devoured by a too consuming object of love.
  This risk of an intense love is felt as being a source of danger by a fairly large number of subjects, the "pregenital" ones according to Maurice Bouvet.[9] For certain subjects, this perception of a danger is accompanied by symptoms of either a psychic (anxiety, aggressiveness, for example) or a somatic (impotency, frigidity, headaches, etc.) nature. In others, this perception is expressed by quasi-preventative behavior, keeping one's distance from the chosen object, engaging in a large number of emotional and affective activities or involvements independently of the principal partner. This defensive strategy then pushes the subject to choose an object unknowingly presenting analogous perceptions. This is why one can observe in these couples the bringing of a third party, who separates and protects, into their relational space.

I shall add Kaës' contribution[10] concerning the *impact of the sibling complex.* For a woman, this can be the choice of the brotherly imago as object of love, which leads her to establish romantic ties with the man who will become her husband. This brother was idealizable as a "complementary narcissistic object," a "masculine and bisexual double." With her husband as substitute for this brother, she reconstitutes this brother–sister couple, which can account for failures in the couple's sexual life and inhibitions connected with this incestuous fantasy. Let me point out that the representation of the narcissistic double and bisexual double would be a form of defense against the difference between the sexes, the difference between generations and the fantasy of castration.

It is appropriate to state that the diverse types of that choice are usually combined and coordinated between partners in accordance in diverse ways.

Unconscious alliances and the structuring of couples

Let us recall what René Kaës[11] has told us about unconscious alliances and their impact on the structuring of couples.

He maintains that to establish the bond, subjects must develop and seal alliances between them that bring together, construct, the "psychic material" and the psychic reality resulting from it. As intersubjective psychic formations, they produce the repressed (through repression) and non-repressed (through rejection, denial, debarment) unconscious, and within it, they perform structuring and defensive functions. All the alliances are sustained by drive investments and unconscious fantasies that function as the dynamic, structural organizers of the bond, something I have already mentioned.

Both the condition and result of these alliances, the mutual identifications perform multiple functions and produce common, shared formations. These unconscious alliances are also processes and means of achieving unconscious aims.

Within the couple, the scene and means for the realization of unconscious desires that none of the subjects could realize alone, Kaës identifies alliances of realization of desire and "defensive pacts" or "denegative pacts" (1989).[12] The latter, he explains, are concluded in order to assure the defensive needs of the subjects when they form a bond and in order to maintain this bond. They are, therefore, to be considered as a mode of resolving intrapsychic conflicts and conflicts traversing a configuration of a bond. Most of the unconscious alliances would be developed in view of dealing with, not only a lack, castration, separation and loss, but especially with destruction, the impossible, the unthinkable. In groups, he tells us, the repressed and non-repressed contents of these alliances are displayed through the formation of symptoms, Freudian slips, enigmatic signs or acts.

Consequently, according to Kaës, the intersubjective bond would organize itself around two related poles: one positively based, the other negatively based on the diverse defensive operations. We therefore observe points of convergence between Lemaire's and Kaës' conceptions when it comes to the dual function of the conjugal bond.

These unconscious alliances themselves depend on "metapsychic guarantors," which provide a framework for the individual psyche, just as "meta-social" guarantors provide a framework for social formations. Finally, each group is characterized by a predominant pair of psychic and socio-cultural organizers serving to stabilize the identity and identifications of its members. This is also something that could be contemplated for couples.

Let us take the example of Judith and Albert

Judith and Albert, both in their thirties, met at their first motorcycle class. Mother of two girls by two different men, working in the teaching profession, Judith appears to be intellectual, cultivated and to exhibit emotional mastery. Albert, the father of a teenage girl, is a "sales person." He appears to be infantile, funny, not very cultivated and particularly impulsive.

In this couple, one finds a combination of several types of choice already mentioned. The reference to the parental couple is positive for Albert and negative for Judith. There is the choice of a defect sought for on a certain level in Albert by Judith, that of affective and emotional fragility particularly finding expression in impulsiveness and violent outbursts that leave an impression upon her and fascinate her. She has a tendency to induce them, unconsciously of course. She in fact takes advantage of these violent outbursts, which are directed against her as well, to find a fantasized satisfaction by identifying with him, all the while confirming for herself that she is better than he is, meaning stronger than he is, and more serious, by criticizing him and condemning him for his transgressions.

One discovers that Judith displays the same dispositions as Albert, but they are repressed and counter-invested. She was never able to explode in the way she fantasized. But in his angry outbursts, Albert identifies with his violent father, whom he feared. He also behaves like an unruly, irascible child, with Judith representing a Superego mother figure making him feel guilty. Actually, after his impulsive outbursts, Albert feels unhappy, ashamed and guilty, like a bad son and a bad, disappointing companion, the whole thing probably satisfying significant masochistic dispositions in him. While Judith is attracted by this fragility on the part of Albert, for him, she represents an ideal figure, through her emotional mastery, her intelligence, her cultivation and her facility in speaking. But she talks too much and floods him with her speeches "which bore him to death." The protection against the risk of intense, invasive love finds expression in him through a regular need to distance himself from her, through his work leading him to absent himself from the couple for days at a time. In her case, this distance finds expression in her need to place between the two of them the fathers of her two daughters, with whom she maintains special friendships, causing Albert to feel jealous. Finally, let me underscore a distinctly marked homosexual component in their couple that finds expression in masculinity on Judith's part, which attracts Albert, as well as a certain femininity on his part, which she finds particularly seductive. They are like two buddies who have a good time together!

The "honeymoon" and crisis in the couple: a psychoanalytical approach

The "honeymoon" phase and the beginnings of a couple's love life

The "honeymoon" phase has a structuring effect on the dyad and is a time of maturation for the two partners. A kind of cancelation exists, an excluding by each partner of any form of aggressiveness toward the other partner, expressed by the intense idealization of the partner and of their love life, and by the greater or lesser sectorial disappearance of psychic limits between the two partners. Each person is more or less felt to be fused with the other person, to be part of him or her. There is a lack of any criticism with regard to the object and a displacement of all aggressiveness toward the outside – third parties forming a common boundary line between the two and a new boundary line between this couple and the world. A "rough sketch" of a symbiotic or fusional couple, a "narcissistic union" in Grunberger's sense[13] playing a very important structuring role for the dyad is then realized.

Nevertheless, the love-object seems only partial, split into good object; the bad, persecuting side is denied, projected upon the outside. This state suggests to me an analogy with the schizo-paranoid position elaborated by Melanie Klein.

Parallels need also be drawn between this phenomenon and the "group illusion," described and conceptualized by Didier Anzieu (1971),[14] which refers to a particular psychic state characterized by a feeling of euphoria that groups in general feel at certain times and are verbally expressed by the members by saying: "We go well together; we make a good group; our leader is a good leader." The group illusion presupposes that the group has been set up as a libidinal object by its members. It replaces the individual's identity with the group identity by affirming that the individuals are identical, and it institutes group narcissism. It would represent a collective defense against the common persecution anxiety, a form of hypomanic defense. Moreover, it would illustrate the functioning of the ideal Ego in groups. There would thus be a substitution of the common ideal Ego for the ideal Ego of each person, meaning that the group would function as ideal Ego in the psychic apparatus of the participants. The counterpart of the group illusion is its fantasies of breaking, in which this group-object is then invested by different forms of destruction drives. Nevertheless, the group illusion fits into a more general process, because "the group just simply fabricates the illusion."

Thus, we could say that for each of the partners, this "honeymoon" phase establishes the couple as a nascent group, object of essentially narcissistic investment inaugurating a "conjugal narcissism" or "conjugal Self," to use Grunberger's expression for individual narcissism.

And, if one were to be so bold as to repeat the analogy with the living being in the process of becoming that the infant represents, drawing inspiration then from what Winnicott has said about this,[15] I would like to suggest that this nascent couple is animated by an "innate creative drive" conferring upon it creative potentialities

Sketching a "natural" history of the couple 63

in connection with the illusion, just as it is also endowed with an innate potential for growth, integration and maturation.

Couple crisis and psychic work of mourning

The crisis process enters in with the disappointment felt by the subject in the face of some presumed failure on the part of the object, which no longer seems to respond to all of his or her desires. Even if the partner or external love-object has not changed, it is the internal love-object that seems to have fallen short, is then felt to be unsatisfactory. As a consequence, it is the psychic reality of the subject that is modified, and not the objective reality of the love-object. This disappointment therefore leads into the processes of the breakdown of idealization and splitting, the return of auto- and hetero-aggressive drives, the reorganization of a genuine natural ambivalence necessary to the good functioning of the object-relation, something which can be hard to bear. This disappointment also awakens the possibility of a new form of criticism, a certain form of testing reality forbidding the pursuance of functioning based on ignorance of a part of the object. The love-object therefore becomes total, and the love relationship, now ambivalent, can therefore give way to a "depressive position" with feelings of guilt, need for reparation, capacity for concern for the other person. Of course, each partner is thrown back upon the painful reality of the alterity of the love-object, of its variability, of its power, of his or her inability to control it and possess it, and also of his or her so narcissistically hurtful dependence upon it.

According to André Ruffiot,[16] the conjugal crisis establishes a form of psychic functioning in the dyad which presents all psychotic virtualities: denial, splittings of the love-object and the Ego into good and bad, combined with a paranoid experience of the internalized partner apprehended as a part of the Ego endangering psychic integrity. The love-object consequently becomes an internal persecutor for each person.

A certain number of defensive processes will be mobilizable in order to avoid and overcome this crisis, such as maintaining the idealization of the love-object in spite of everything, accompanied by a split in virtue of which the good object is at the origin of the couple, and the bad object is attributed to external factors, which leads to aggressive behaviors of a projective kind with regard to third parties and to possessive behaviors with regard to the love-object. Moreover, there is aggressive behavior directed toward the object avoiding self-criticism. These auto- and hetero-behaviors produce mutual narcissistic disconfirmation between the two partners.

In the clinical approach to couples, I shall distinguish between two orders of causality determining the onset of a crisis: on the one hand, external events, potentially critical stages and times of trial, experienced and lived through by each or both spouses in the course of their time together; on the other hand, the maturing of one of the members, which "pushes" him or her to desire secondarily the drive satisfaction against which he or she had protected him- or herself in choosing his or her partner in the beginning. This is the return of what had been repressed (Œdipus complex, homosexuality and pregenital drives), which leads one to reproach one's partner for what one had appreciated so greatly in him or her in the beginning.

Potentially critical stages and times of trial in the life of the couple

Allow me to cite some of these potentially critical times of trial and stages that will represent narcissistic wounds, mourning, traumas, painful events, but also happy ones – the latter capable of producing œdipal guilt in its perpetrator and envy in the partner, triggering a conjugal critical state. All these situations will be capable of reactivating psychic conflicts, multiple anxieties, pregenital (persecution, depressive) and œdipal especially, but will also satisfy desires for accomplishment, narcissistic completeness, fantasies of omnipotence: living together, or moving into a common space (their fantasized habitat as an imaginary common body); institutionalizing the couple through marriage or civil union; presenting each of the partners to families and to friends; formulating the desire and making plans to have a child, or the lack of such a desire in one of the two; the birth of the first child, or of subsequent children, therefore the transition from couple to family and the potentially conflictual differentiation between parental couple and couple in love or conjugal couple; possible later births or the enlargement of the family, and also the mourning of other desired births, miscarriages, abortions; the childless couple owing to the couple's sterility; the stages of the family cycle, in particular, the children's adolescent years and the reactivation of the parents' œdipal conflict; personal successes and failures – be they professional, relational, involving leisure activities, but also conjugal or familial – multiple losses; physical issues occurring in one of the partners, the circumstances and determinant factors of which would also need to be thought through within the context of conjugal functioning, and its impact on each partner's psychic economy. In return, we could take into consideration: the impact of these individual physical issues on the economic and dynamic aspects of the couple; as well as serious illnesses affecting the couple's children and having their impact on the parental couple and the family dynamic; the children's leaving home; the end of the professional activity of one, then both, of the partners determining the loss of a major sublimational activity having multiple repercussions on the psychic economy of the retiree and his or her couple; the couple finding themselves *tête-à-tête*; the marrying of the children, the birth of grandchildren, the couple's becoming "grandparental."

Extra-conjugal acting: factor of crisis and/or solution symptomatic of a crisis?

"Extra-conjugal acting" or relationships or extra-conjugal love affairs can emerge at different times in the life of the couple, in the man and/or in the woman.

Indeed, one or the other can arise preventatively, so as to limit the density of the love relationship from the beginning, as a means of protection against pregenital fantasies such as that of engulfment, of being devoured by the love-object and that of being invaded by the couple-object, something which leads to the multiplication of secondary partners.

Apart from a critical period – individual or conjugal – if one partner lets the other see and know in an exhibitionistic way, this can be part of a perverse kind of game – as exhibitionistic-voyeuristic as it is sado-masochistic – with the other partner, which the latter can implicitly accept or reject. In the case of acceptance, one partner may derive fantasized satisfaction by identifying with the other partner, in which case this scenario would then respond to an unconscious distribution of roles, in which one partner is appointed to act out the other's fantasy (Kaës' phoric function),[17] both experiencing two different modes of gratification: direct and fantasized. However, if the unfaithful partner remains secretive, without any notable conjugal dimension, this could take on more individual symptomatic significance, such as a defensive modality against castration anxiety, disturbed primary oral relation being treated by a compulsive genital relationship, a desire for conquest, or the fear of incestuous fantasy. It may also be understandable in terms of the beginnings of dissatisfaction, with the impossibility of introducing perverse components into the conjugal erotic life, and therefore of satisfying certain fantasies.

In a period of individual and/or conjugal crisis, if there is personal fragilization, depressiveness, or narcissistic disconfirmation by the partner, he or she may seek this lost narcissistic reassurance and/or this confirmation in someone else. In this case, the quest for narcissistic input and confirmation prevails over erotic gratification.

There may be advantages in this, notably a relibidinization of conjugal bonds, revitalizing the couple settled into a fatal state of extinction. But one may also seek lost love that is impossible to re-experience with one's partner, that "honeymoon," that largely dampened "group illusion." The erotic then combines with the narcissistic.

This acting, or this affair, can also have a hostile aim, seeking to discredit the other person, who becomes an object of hate, a prop for the projection of bad and rejected parts of oneself.

It may occur after the birth of a child or children, the lovers having become parents, something implying disruption of the couple's libidinal economy, the new mother overinvesting in her child or children, with a possible, relative disinvestment – erotic as well as narcissistic – on the part of her partner, whose new role as father may awaken the fear of incestuous fantasy, and this could be so, reciprocally, for the man.

There is also a possible desire in the "unfaithful" partner to free him- or herself from the partner's control and domination, therefore, a desire for separation-individuation, emancipation, but above all for subjectivization, which adopts a genitalized, but also sadomasochistic, erotic language. What cannot be verbalized will be expressed by this type of erotic acting in particular.

66 Sketching a "natural" history of the couple

Finally, let me mention the existence in a heterosexual conjugal partner of extra-conjugal acting or affairs with homosexual partners. Light can be shed on this complex situation by looking at the drive economy of every subject and the rearranging it undergoes in the course of the events of his or her life, underlain by the mobility of his or her libidinal investments—both homosexual and heterosexual. Other approaches to understanding this matter will quite obviously need to be investigated.

Three post-critical evolving possibilities identified by Jean-Georges Lemaire

In certain cases, the partner's disinvestment and mutual aggressiveness continue to grow and lead to separation and the death of the couple.

At other times, one sees a certain number of post-critical reactions organizing themselves within the couple, the partners behaving as if to dismiss any possible source of new conflicts. But, unable to invest themselves mutually and organize new "collusions," they try to protect their relationship by strictly limiting all investments external to the couple itself, even if it means limiting their own personal fulfillment. It is often through the intermediary of the children that a new mode of functioning of the couple – one revolving around their difficulties, and their pathology, especially – finds itself mediated. A certain number of fantasies and affects that no longer flow freely between the partners are from then on polarized around the child. In particular, the couple may be kept stable at the price of the common rejection of the child, by displacing both partners' hatred – initially directed against themselves – upon it, something which will be the cause of serious disturbances in its evolution.

Finally, in a third and greater number of cases, the couple reorganizes new bonds, whence comes the dynamic, re-creative effect of the crisis, even when it has been experienced by the partners as a painful, destructive phenomenon. Turning to Anzieu for inspiration, we could envisage the existence of oscillations between the two poles of the "group illusion" and "fantasies of breaking" in the life of a couple as a group, the couple in crisis being experienced by its members as a bad, persecuting and castrating object against which one must protect oneself. Nevertheless, the crisis has a maturing effect, both on the intersubjective relationship – calling upon the partners' creativity in realizing beneficial rearrangements – and on the "conjugal group," which must preserve a sufficient level of narcissistic investment.

This is why, according to Lemaire, the human couple must be considered functionally as a structured whole, paced by alternations of phases marked in each individual by idealizing splittings and constantly renewed work of mourning the idealized object. The human couple experiences processes of organization–disorganization and reorganization of interrelationships between the partners that lends it an equilibrium that is dynamic in nature. Nevertheless, it is a matter of an intersubjective approach to the couple and not of a group approach, which it would be desirable to associate with it.[18]

Living together, or developing a conjugal culture and identity

Living together implies the creation of a common, shared space-time that will inevitably be in a state of tension with that of the partners' separate, differentiated space-times. It is a matter of fields of fantasized fomentation and flow, of multiple symbolizations and sublimations within which individual and conjugal compromise formations will be worked out, finding expression in: the creation and investment of both common, shared and differentiated, separate activities (professional, extraprofessional, leisure activities); the elaboration of common, unshared representations and ideas (those of the man and of the woman, of their respective roles within the couple, of their relationships within the couple, those of the couple, inspired by their respective families, those of the family, in particular); the establishment of stable, variable forms of communication, of norms of conduct, of rules of domestic organization and functioning – mobilizing both partners' anality – of common ideals and values, of mythical tales, of ritual activities evolving into habits, sexuality figuring among them, the establishment of conjugal institutions.

We can also take into consideration the organization of a conjugal economy involving income, budget, expenditures and modes of consumption, the investment of conduct regarding savings. The distribution of power, the ways of exercising it and its differentiated sectors would also need to be taken into consideration. To be mentioned are the modes of investment and the conscious and unconscious representations of their habitat, "the couple's bodily envelope," interplay of investments among their couple, sphere of intimacy, its boundaries and the external world, the relationships between the private couple/public couple and their possible splitting. Finally, the investment of time, shared and not shared, their individual and common (past, present, future) temporality are also significant areas of conjugal life. This conjugal culture will produce an identity proper to the couple, a conjugal, narcissistically invested identity reflecting the existence of common, shared psychic agencies such as: the "conjugal Self," narcissistic agency and reservoir of conjugal drives, a place of pooling personal energies; the "conjugal Ego" involved in the couple's everyday socio-cultural reality and *animating* the *work couple*; and finally, the formations of the Ideal and the Superego.

With a view toward making this development of a conjugal culture and identity intelligible, I shall take a look at a pluridisciplinary exploration of certain particular areas: the organization of domestic life and the definition of roles; communication and its modalities; conflicts; conjugal rhythms; and, finally, the sexuality that plays such a central role in couples' lives nowadays.

68 Sketching a "natural" history of the couple

The organization of domestic life, the definition of roles and the distribution of personal territories

A sociological approach

A couple's domestic organization cannot be understood outside the dynamic involved in the elementary, routine behavior upon which it is based, falling within the entirety of tasks needing to be performed, which are represented differently for the partners: lofty, for real estate projects and child raising; humble even degrading for the more automatic and repetitive tasks (putting things away and cleaning the house); rather nuanced for others, such as cooking. However, since the work of couples and families changes with the historical context, Jean-Claude Kaufmann has observed in our times a continual trend toward externalization. An increasing number of activities are being outsourced and socialized, being taken over by the public sector, associations, the service sector, whence comes the question of what may be outsourced and what must not be.[19]

In addition, inquiring into the significance of this domestic work, Kaufmann considers that the performance of these multiple tasks greatly contributes to the daily construction of conjugal relationships and to that of the identities of the partners "socialized" in the couple. I see this notion of domestic work as falling into the framework of the *work couple*, a concept inspired by Bion's notion of "work group," later adopted by Anzieu. I shall come back to this.

What about personal territories? The idea of egalitarian sharing of domestic tasks being very recent, the roles must first be worked out together. Who is supposed to do what? Distribution in terms of personal territories has proved to be dominant (cooking for one partner, cleaning for the other, for example), and this does not in theory seem incompatible with the idea of equality. However, despite this egalitarian model, Kaufmann sees progress toward a more equitable, concrete distribution of domestic tasks as only taking place extremely slowly. He observes, then, a form of complementarity resulting from two factors: the difference between the sexes, tending to lead, depending upon whether one is a man or a woman, to two contrasting sectors of the domestic arrangement; and conjugal functioning, which would be conducive to reinforcing certain contrasts, thus enabling partners to mark out personal territories better and to strengthen each one's "coherence of identity." It is especially dependent upon the existence of gender specificity in two areas: that of housework for the woman, that of the role of provider for the man.

As a consequence, the precise defining of roles in the course of the conjugal cycle is a quite complex and shifting process, which plays out at the intersection of the internalization of cultural and parental models and the specific dynamic of the intersubjective relationship. The identity of any couple also stands out in the way they distribute roles within the domestic context.

A psychoanalytical approach

What might a psychoanalyst have to say on this matter?

Setting up the organization of domestic work – according to Grunberger's thoughts[20] on the matter – calls upon the partners' anality, but also upon capacities for investment of the tasks to be performed, narcissistic in nature – the inside of the home being conceived of as an extension of oneself and as the couple's bodily envelope, a shared, common narcissistic object – but also sublimated sadistic-anal and homosexual in nature. The post-œdipal sexual identifications with parental figures, with their respective domestic roles and modes of relating, but also counter-identifications with them, would contribute to structuring the distribution of domestic roles and the distribution of personal territories, as well as the underlying conjugal flow of fantasies and the multiple meanings that performing these tasks represents within the intersubjective relationship and the framework of the group reality. Narcissistic confirmation can be expected from this. A form of seduction could be at work, as well as procured sublimated pregenital satisfactions.

Moreover, as Bion noticed, followed in that by Anzieu, this area of conjugal life mobilizes one of the two levels of functioning of every couple, the *work couple* or *technical pole*, interacting with the *basic couple* or *fantasized pole*.

In performing common tasks, this *work couple* would display the characteristics of the Ego governed by the reality principle and animated by the logic of the functioning of secondary psychic processes. Nevertheless, this conscious cooperation is quite obviously not exclusively rational, because it is also pervaded, even disturbed by a conscious and unconscious, fantasized, emotional flow that can be as stimulating as it is paralyzing.

Regarding the sources and forms of energy employed, apart from the sublimated libidinal energy mentioned above, would it be pertinent to envisage the participation of what is called the actual energy of functions or instinct of self-preservation in the service of the couple's survival?

The diverse forms and the style of conjugal communication

A sociological approach

Along with the sociologists, I shall differentiate between the level of exchanges of "goods and services" and the complexity of their "flow," and that of the forms and levels of communication.

Every day, a quantity of varied and diverse "goods and services" circulate within the couple, going back and forth from one partner to the other, weaving the conjugal fabric. Sociologists have highlighted rules of structuring and interplay of complementarity defined especially by the positions occupied by the two partners. So it is that, depending on the social milieu and, above all, depending on gender, men and women do not expect the same "goods and services": men would rather look for physical, sexual attractiveness and selfish, immediate emotional support. More than women, they would consider their companion to be their best friend, while women would more readily seek economic capital, sentiment and intimate communication, the emotional support being integrated in this form.

Fitting into a complex intersubjective dynamic, these exchanges would therefore yield "collective gains and losses," and both conjugal satisfaction and dissatisfaction would serve to regulate this, according to Kaufmann.

70 Sketching a "natural" history of the couple

The forms, channels, messages and levels of communication are diverse, stable for certain of its aspects and variable for others, depending on the stages of the couple's life together, the circumstances of daily life, the partners' affective and emotional states, especially.

Particularly interested in messages, Kaufmann has us observe, contrary to received wisdom, that it is not possible to speak in just any way and about just anything at all in a couple, but very constraining rules structure and limit communicational exchanges.[21] To understand them, he invites us to identify different types of messages beforehand.

Quantitatively speaking, the most important of these are the ordinary conversations of daily life about frivolous or more important subjects. This is the principal tool enabling partners to nurture the intersubjective relationship, but also to construct, produce and maintain the couple's group reality, as well as to structure and affirm its identity. Nevertheless, with certain statements, one slips from this simple chatting into a second type of message, within a context of informal, verbalized "reveries," which concern possible changes of orientation, the elaboration of projects leading to possible decision-makings by the *work couple.*

The third type would readily deal with the affective dimension of the conjugal relationship, bearing witness to a tender, loving investment on the part of another person, to a "capacity for concern for the other person," and to joint narcissistic confirmation.

The fourth type concerns managing dissatisfaction and conflicts, angry words and "cooler" explanations of disagreements.

The fifth type pertains to attempts to analyze the conjugal relationship itself, assessments of it, and possible changes to undertake. This is obviously the most difficult to apply, because there is a danger it will call into question certain foundations of the couple.

The ways of expressing oneself differ in accordance with the types of messages. The verbal communication can be variable and mimetic-gestural, non-verbal communication more especially used in certain affective and relational contexts.

Kaufmann has detected a manifestation of the difference between the sexes in this conjugal area of communication. Indeed, according to him, men and women do not express themselves in the same manner. Thus, women much more frequently initiate a conversation about their couple and family, which is frequently brought to an end by men on account of their position, while these same subjects brought up less frequently by men actually come to be expanded upon. Women talk more because they would have more to say and to ask. Less centered on the couple, men "flee into silence" and resort more to "secret withdrawal." Their conversation within the couple is more neutral and deals more with public facts. Women who have more strictly conjugal expectations are led to engage in less neutral communication more often carried to extremes: the positive extreme, tied to their propensity toward affectivity (more frequent laughter and smiles); the negative extreme (recriminations), tied to their requirements for explanations regarding their expectations. For the same reason, women send clearer, better understood messages.

A psychoanalytical approach

With its multiple forms, levels and nuances of functioning, communication plays a role in creating the couple, in structuring the roles and identities of the two partners within the intersubjective relationship, as well as in producing the "nourishing material" of conjugal reality, in giving it its "existential consistency." It most obviously has "pragmatic" functions, which I shall not discuss. I shall in fact only provide some information about certain of its groupal, intersubjective aspects. Certain forms of communication will be more particularly invested by each of the partners within the context of an unconscious distribution of roles, then procuring them direct and indirect fantasized satisfactions. In verbal communication, the phoric function of message-bearer will therefore be able to be fulfilled by one of the two, as well as that of the "fantasy-bearer" and that of "action bearer." Very invested in one party, verbal communication will therefore be able to "resonate" with the insufficient investment in it by the other person who, for diverse unconscious reasons, will invest more willingly in another visual, tactile, mimetic-gestural, non-verbal form, but also in action as a communicational language. Among these unconscious reasons, certain individual and cultural representations will associate verbal communication with femininity and action with masculinity. For neurotic reasons, when too invested erotically, verbal communication will be the object of possible inhibition by way of an unconscious compromise. Within the context of conjugal fantasy life dominated by symbiotic and fusional representations, this form of communication may also be experienced as a threat to the psychic integrity of each partner, something which leads to restricting it, therefore, to impoverishing the diverse levels of the conjugal relationship. The sadistic-anal, aggressive dimension – often projective in nature – will be able to be prevalent within a context of conjugal crisis that it is difficult to be able to verbalize. This responds to and accompanies mutual narcissistic disconfirmation that may evolve toward conjugal violence. Fantasies of the reactivated schizo-paranoid position, as well as that of the "sadistic primal scene" would probably underlie this.

Communication in times of conflict will respond to a certain type of conjointly worked out scenario that will procure gratifications of a narcissistic nature – through the reassertion of "individualities," the reinforcement of their psychic boundaries – and of a pregenital, sadistic-anal and phallic nature for each partner within this context of "reorganizing confrontation." It will enable them to make "adjustments" on three levels: groupal, intersubjective and intrapsychic-individual.

Apart from the habitual style of communication established by the couple, one of its identity components, it will be able to evolve in the course of their life together owing to changes experienced by one or both partners, but it will also be the object of variations inherent in existential events, in each one's emotional fluctuations, determining the choice of a certain form, or a certain category, or a certain type of message rather than other ones. Each couple in fact also creates, constitutes its own communicational repertory in which it chooses, in accordance with different factors, the modalities adequate to the situations.

72 Sketching a "natural" history of the couple

The conflicts

A sociological approach

The forms and causes of conjugal conflict are diverse. Dona Francescato (1992),[22] an Italian sociologist cited by Kaufmann, has identified two principal causes: the difficult handling of differences between partners and disenchantment in love.

Difference would not in itself be problematic given, as I have already explained, the initial search for complementarity in the partners. It only becomes so when it finds expression in opposing personal interests between partners, in divergent ideas about the conjugal project or in "annoyance, irritation" felt in daily life before the painful reality of differences in their ways of doing things, thinking and feeling. So Francescato maintains that the majority of conflicts arise through the abrupt revelation of the unacceptability of the partner's way of doing things, which throws the couple into crisis.

Kaufmann explains the existence of a great deal of variability in the effects of this confrontation of conjugal differences by the contradictory nature of identity work. The couple, he considers, is actually an extension of oneself, an immersion of the I in something concrete experienced by two people, at the same time as being a loving refusal to criticize one's partner, whence comes the capacity for negating differences. But, the individual cannot fail to resurface through the reassertion of his or her own boundaries. The almost pleasant liberating aspect of the conflict is often tied to this simple, reassuring manifestation of the individual self (generally combining with a claim made in terms of personal interests), which cannot, however, repeat itself too often, without risking breaking up the couple. The hesitation is therefore ongoing, making managing conjugal contradictions very complex.[23] Inspired by, or connecting up with, the ideas of Lemaire in particular, this approach is much more psycho-sociological than strictly sociological.

In contrast, disenchantment with love would appear to be much simpler. Conjugal cycles in fact evolve toward the transformation of the early intense feeling of love into forms of tenderness, complicity and generosity, whence comes an experience of loss and nostalgia and the need to undertake mourning work. Women would feel the loss of intimacy in conjugal communication more keenly, while men would complain about the sexual loss – the female partner seeming less desirable, or feeling less interested, sexually rejecting her partner more or less explicitly.

Kaufmann has further observed that for some decades, the place of conflict has changed owing to the growing instability of couples because from now on the conflict would be liable to lead to the breakup of the couple, while in the past, conflict was part of an institutionally controlled, compulsorily stable and lasting union. It could, nevertheless, be violent provided that it did not call into question the choice of partner. However, nowadays, conjugal violence cannot develop without self-control, without running the risk of triggering a possible breakup. So, how does one enter into conflict without calling the couple into question? Real, more or less ritualized, domestic disputes develop and, having obvious regulative effects, this ritualization will avoid or attempt to prevent the dangers of breakup. As modes of expression and dealing with dissatisfaction, these conflicts function not only as a form of "discharge," but also as an indication of certain problems, of their possible clarification being able to evolve toward changes beneficial to the couple and to each of the two partners.

A psychoanalytical approach

Let us remember that all conjugal reality is dynamic and therefore structurally conflictual. Indeed, the construction, then the durability of a couple, assume negotiation, the attenuation, even the denial of its diverse primordial conflictualities between: Ego/love-object, Ego/couple-object; identity/alterity; narcissism/objectality; Eros/instinct of destruction; self-preservation/sexuality; pregenitality/genitality; male/female; psychic bisexuality/sexual identity, couple/external reality, private couple/public couple, in particular. Intrapsychic and intersubjective compromises mobilizing diverse defensive processes – themselves dynamic and economic in nature, meaning shifting, variable, and therefore fragile – will necessarily have to be at work. This is why a psychoanalytic understanding of conjugal conflicts must imperatively first conceive of every couple as a living reality, and therefore dynamic, economic and topographical, immersed in a world external to it, source of beneficial and pernicious phenomena. Inadequate compromises, the prevalence of "quantitative" economic factors through a lack of mastery of individual and/or conjugal critical situations, for example, will be a determinant factor in individual and/or conjugal psychic suffering that will find expression in the emergence of "conjugal conflicts" localizing themselves on one or several levels of conjugal reality: psychic, sexual-bodily, and socio-cultural. They will assume different variable or quite regular forms evolving toward a ritualization. They will be manifest, utilizing diversified modes of communication, but will also be latent, unconscious obstacles hindering their exteriorization. The psychoanalyst will be able to fantasize about their existence through the counter-transferential feelings of tension, heaviness, even boredom, experienced in consultation.

While they testify to a "noisiness" of the essential conflictual dynamic of every couple, they also reveal more or less pronounced failures of *couple work*, a concept I shall present in a later chapter.

Among identifiable functions, Lemaire discusses the function of setting boundaries and of strengthening each partner's individual, insufficient boundaries. The endangered narcissistic and identity assertion is expressed in that way. But it can also be a matter of a means of expressing the need for a change in conjugal functioning, whence comes its function as a mutative, reorganizing phase of the couple and of each partner's relationship to their couple-object, calling upon their creativity, in the service of their self-preservation.

The couple's erotic life or sexuality

An anthropological perspective

First, let me introduce some basic generalities about sexuality in connection with Françoise Héritier's work.

She tells us that in traditional societies, notably African societies, the right to sexual relationships and to reproduction is appropriated by a sexually active generation, which monopolizes it and alone will consent, through appropriate rituals and "mystic consent," to its progressive dispossession. So it is that the son's "vital force" comes from the decline in the father's, the girl's fecundity from the decline in the mother's. One must act in such a way that none of the parties present "overtakes" the others. That would definitely be an offense against the ancestors and the social law regulating the harmonious, orderly succession of generations, she explains.[24] Infringing upon this rule would then be punished either socially or "mystically."

A sociological perspective

According to Michel Bozon, and in keeping with the views of other specialists, sexuality is neither explained by sexuality, nor by biology. Its transformations over the course of time must be viewed in relation to other social transformations, and comparisons of sexual conducts in different countries need to be connected with social differences in those countries, rooted in history. Let us remember with Bozon the major changes that took place during last decades of the twentieth century, which may be characterized by a decline in the threefold identification of sexuality with reproduction, with the marriage institution and with heterosexuality, as well as by the emergence of numerous paradoxical injunctions which individuals must come to terms with through all sorts of compromise. Among these, I might mention those of reconciling the requirement of reciprocity and that of individual self-fulfillment, of simultaneously displaying spontaneity and self-control, or demonstrating both flexibility in situations and self-consistency.

In addition, Bozon has us observe that in every country sexuality evolves in distinct ways tied to its social history and the frameworks and meanings it has developed. The principal differences would be inherent in the organization of marriage, in the "social organization of ages," and in the system of relationships between the sexes. Thus, in the southern European countries, the traditional separation of the world of women and that of men goes hand in hand with much less participation by women in the job market, a certain solidity in the institution of marriage, a very non-egalitarian distribution of responsibilities in the home and a double standard for sexual behavior, which manifests itself in pronounced differences in the age of sexual initiation. Inversely, the Nordic countries are characterized by convergence in the behavior of men and women in all these areas and by a decline in marriage.

Along with Bozon, let us look at some paradigmatic aspects of contemporary sexuality and their impact on couples.

DISSOCIATING SEXUALITY–PROCREATION

At the heart of the sphere of intimacy and affectivity, which has greatly expanded over the course of time, sexuality has emerged as a personal practice basic to the construction of the subject, within which procreation occupies a specific, but limited, space. The "second contraceptive revolution" that has been taking place since the 1960s has then brought with it a reversal in the manner of viewing fecundity, since that time thought of as a personal project, prepared for by two people, that could be coordinated with other projects. Technologization that alters the nature of sexuality, medically assisted procreation (artificial insemination, in-vitro fertilization) represents a further step in this process of dissociating sexuality and procreation

MEDICALIZATION AND THE PSYCHOLOGIZATION OF SEXUALITY

In the contemporary experience of sexuality, the discourse and practice of medicine, psychology and sexology have taken an essential place in the origination of new normative models of conduct, such as the obligation to be concerned about the functioning of one's sexuality, which since the 1960s, through the work of Masters and Johnson,[25] has become a source of personal and collective well-being.

THE COURSE OF THE COUPLE'S SEXUAL LIFE

Bozon considers that the sexuality of couples goes through phases that follow a fairly regular course: the beginning phase and the phase called stabilization.

The beginning phase, which corresponds to the very first years of life together, is characterized by intense sexual activity with a varied repertory, according particular importance to sexual exclusivity, and therefore to fidelity. Moreover, let us remember that this sexual activity contributes to the very construction of the couple as an intersubjective relationship and group reality.

During the phase termed stabilization, which begins after some years have passed, sexual activity progressively evolves into a habitual way of sustaining the couple, a private ritual that periodically and symbolically reaffirms the couple' existence. Abatement of feelings of love, the less frequent confluence of reciprocal sexual desires, the impact of the significant investment in parenthood and professional life, in particular, contribute to lessening conjugal sexual activity, which in spite of its symbolic significance becomes less central for each partner. Likewise, periods of absence of desire grow more frequent. Moreover, when they do take place, extra-conjugal relations have less serious consequences on the future of the couple than at the very beginning.

76 Sketching a "natural" history of the couple

Elements of differentiation of the sexes in this area of contemporary sexuality

The coming closer together of the courses of the lives of men and women and their sexual attitudes is observable nowadays in most developed countries, asserting itself more forcefully in northern Europe than in Latin countries. It involves a retreat from the traditional passivity in love that was expected of women and the opening up of new opportunities for them. Nevertheless, that does not mean that the gap between what they experience has been closing in as neat a way, something which also depends upon power relationships between partners, and society's judgments of their behavior.

Procreation has proved to be a decisive threshold to cross in this transition from the "convergent nascent couple" to the "divergent stabilized couple." And it is among couples with very young children that the gap between the expectations of men and women is the greatest, Bozon maintains.

The manner in which sexuality is lived is expressed in terms of social representations that clearly distinguish between what is female and what is male, thus contrasting female sexuality – mainly thought of in terms of affectivity, relationships, procreation and conjugality – with male sexuality mostly thought of on the level of natural needs, individual desire and pleasure. Bozon deems that, in spite of a considerable opening up of possibilities for Western women, both in the ways in which sexuality is portrayed and the ways it is practiced, the sexual sphere remains the bastion of quiet inegalitarianism, in which differences and asymmetry between the sexes seem to be the very condition of the good realization of sexual interaction.[26]

A psychoanalytical approach

I therefore understand human sexuality to be, all at once, "biocorporeal sexuality," "socio-sexuality" and psychosexuality, the major significance of which I am going to show.

Indeed, the couple's sexuality – fundamentally conflictual and object of varying degrees of investment by each partner and by the couple itself over the course of time – mobilizes the different links in the "erotic chain" defined by Green: the flows of aggressive, erotic, tender and narcissistic investments, the states of pleasure–unpleasure, the libido's pregenital and genital components, the diverse coupling of the psychosexuality, the bisexuality of each of the partners, the specification of male and female desires fed by conscious and unconscious representations laden with affects, pregenital fantasies (of subject/object fusion, bisexuality, engulfment, being devoured, for example) and œdipal fantasies (of seduction, primal scene and castration, incestuous fantasy) causing multiple anxieties, themselves pregenital and œdipal, the interplay of cross-identifications, especially. The whole can be at work in the act of love, but certain of these aspects will be prevalent depending on the moments, the periods, stages of life and the life story of each of the couples. As a consequence, sexuality is pregenital and genital, heterosexual and/or homosexual, direct, inhibited in its instinctual aim, or

Sketching a "natural" history of the couple 77

indirect, fantasized, sublimated and symbolized. A style of sexual life or of couple sexuality will thus be co-invented by the two partners while possibly evolving.

Apart from the direct instinctual satisfactions, allow me to mention the narcissistic satisfaction deriving from the state of completeness experienced in this "narcissistic union" that enables one to perform the genital sexual act. Indeed, the latter lives out the fantasy of an imaginary common body – a narcissistic fantasy structuring the couple as a groupal psychic entity – and that of bisexuality, fantasy of omnipotence denying the difference between the sexes, as well as any difference at all.

Concerning sexual disorders, let me point out their over-determination, which combines group, intersubjective and individual meanings. The intersubjective interpretation will bring into play the notion of phoric function already discussed with the "symptom-bearer." Allow me to mention certain well-known significations: the existence of incestuous fantasies, a limitation of the density of the relationship and, on that level, a danger of depersonalizing fusion, of fantasies of engulfment and being devoured, the refusal to submit to the other person's desires, the fear of abandoning oneself, as well as of active unconscious fantasies of a dangerous, destructive penis in the woman and a dangerous vagina in the man.

The presentation of a unified discourse on the subject being inconceivable, it seems to me more interesting to discuss the theoretical elaborations by certain specialists of aspects of sexuality that will afford us a glimpse of the full complexity of that vast field.

Thus, with Michel Fain and Denise Braunschweig,[27] let us take a look at the difficult questions surrounding the characterization of desire and erotic sexuality within the context of an antagonist relationship with the sexuality-discharge and an aspiration toward narcissistic dedifferentiation-fusion

They maintain that the genesis of the organization of desire is based on twofold restraint: restraining representation of the absent object and restraining the immediate need for discharge, indispensable to cultivating the pleasure of restraining representation of the object (the pleasure of desire). An auto-erotic nucleus of a retentive kind would thus enter into the structure of the desire and prelude the pleasure of retention proper to the anal stage, the condition of which is the avoidance of narcissistic fusion. It is then a matter of reintroducing desire's antithetical element, narcissism, into its elaboration.

The erotic aspect of sexual relations would then consist of a game whose goal would be to maintain sexual desire at its highest level for an optimal amount of time. And, Fain and Braunschweig consider that it is much more this feeling of potential liberation than the real exercising of liberation that would constitute the essence of sexual eroticism.

They detect a contradiction at work within a couple in love including, on the one hand, a mutual projection of narcissisms and an aspiration to narcissistic fusion with a desire for dedifferentiation of the partners and, on the other hand, an aspiration to maintain erotic desire, endowed sometimes with attractive partial tendencies (sadism, masochism, for example), for the necessary and sufficient time, so that the couple acquires the feeling of potential liberation from the expression of desire. Once this feeling has been experienced, the idea of becoming one takes on completely different meaning. And the orgasm, the meeting place of these two antagonistic aims, then appears to be the moment bringing this structural contradiction to an end.

Then, I shall expand upon Jacqueline Schaeffer's particularly original approach (1997,[28] 2002,[29] 2007[30]), which reveals to us all the richness and complexity of the sexuality of couples, placing it into the dual context of the conflictual existence of each of the partners, male and female, and that of the difference between the sexes.

In the first place, she considers that, throughout their lives, both women and men experience inevitable antagonism involving three poles, erotic sexual life, parenthood and social fulfillment, and within a couple, the meeting and organization of the antagonisms of each party are established according to diverse modalities. She observes that in the woman, the antagonism involving the erotic, motherhood and her social achievement, phallic in meaning, is particularly conflictual and ongoing, unlike that of the man, for whom libidinal development, the erotic and social fulfillment follow the same course, that of motivity, conquest and phallic performance.

Then, she hypothesizes that the erotic encounter between a man and a woman, "sexuality for pleasure," is a matter of authentic psychic work involving, especially, the joint elaboration of male and female that mutually "genitalize" in an asymmetry constitutive of the difference between the sexes, something which would be achievable in each partner using "female work," combined in the woman with her erotic masochism.

In women, Schaeffer considers, this work lies in overcoming a conflict constitutive of female sexuality. Women want two conflicting things. *Her sex requires defeat; her Ego hates it.*[31] Provided that his Ego has been able to comply with the constant impulse of the libido, the lover is going to bring that into the woman's body in order to open, reveal the "feminine." And, it is in revealing the woman's vagina that the man, identified then with the libidinal impulse, will be able to tear the woman away from her auto-eroticism and her pregenital mother. This is the reason why access to her genitality is both easier – because she is helped by the man – and more problematic than that of the man – because the woman expects her pleasure to come from the man. This is what makes her dependent, more threatened by the loss of the sexual object than by the loss of a sexual organ.

In men, this "female work" consists in letting the constant libidinal impulse take hold of his penis, in abandoning himself to it and to the sexual object, the sole genuine access to sexual pleasure, which means the capacity to desire a woman, with a "libidinal penis," which will lead him to the discovery and creation of the woman's "feminine." Nevertheless, he will have to let go of his anal and phallic defenses temporarily and not be terrorized by fantasies linked to the danger of the body of the mother-woman. Consequently, the man gains access to the masculine when he becomes what possesses him, that is to say, the constant impulse.

The dissymmetry of the difference between the sexes is enriched by identifications. The man will in turn experience himself as dominated by the woman's capacity to submit to "defeat."

Thus, we understand better what this psychic work of the two partners consists of, which enables them to live a "sexuality of pleasure" relating a "masculine" and a "feminine" in asymmetry constituting the difference between the sexes. It is an experience of "drive introjection" and expansion of the Ego, which is therefore integrative, but also a mutative experience of objectal, narcissistic reorganization.

The couple and their desire for a child

Some anthropological elements

Françoise Héritier thinks that in traditional societies children are not desired as an object of pure desire and appropriation, as a consumer good and as representing some affective investment by the couple or the individual, even if they are economic capital and life insurance. It is more a matter of a desire and duty to have descendants, comparable to a desire and duty to achieve something, rather than a desire for a child. Not transmitting life is breaking a chain of which no one person is the final link, and it is, moreover, barring one's access to the status of ancestor. Thus, marriage and procreation are duties toward those who have gone before us in life. According to this extremely widespread type of view, the desire for a child would above all be an eminently social desire for achievement transmitted through descendants who will preserve the memory of the dead and will worship them in the necessary way. From this perspective, both sterility and the death of children are viewed of as biological misfortunes of the highest order.

The psychoanalytic perspective

Let us remember that the family fantasy underlying the family project is implicit or explicit in every couple.

The fundamentally ambivalent and conflictualized desire for a child is narcissistic and objectal. One desires a child for oneself, desires a child from another person: "I want to have a child by you," "have my child," "let's have a child." The difference between the sexes being particularly pronounced in this area, the psychic polysemy of this desire is rich and complex. Nevertheless, each one's Œdipus constitutes one of the fundamental bases of the desire for a child. In the woman, as in the man, it is a matter of examining the meaning of the desire for a child within the context of their conjugal and individual existential itinerary, of situating its place among their diverse objects of personal and common investments, but also the child's or children's function(s) within the conjugal dynamic and economy.

In women, I shall look at the narcissistic component of this desire conferring upon them a feeling of fullness and completeness, its phallic component filling their female void, but also its objectal, erotic dimension and with its maternal and paternal œdipal resonances. In *Les bébés de l'inconscient, Le psychanalyste face aux stérilités féminines aujourd'hui*, Sylvie Faure-Pragier[32] observed that in Freud's writings before 1924 (*The Dissolution of the Œdipus Complex*),[33] the girl's desire for a child would correspond to the natural expression of feelings for her father, would be the child of incestuous fantasy. From the time of the "turn" made in 1925 in *Some Psychical Consequences of the Anatomical Distinction between the Sexes*,[34] then later in *Female Sexuality*[35] in 1931 and *"Femininity"*[36] in 1933, this desire for a child becomes a substitute for the desire for a penis.

In men, the narcissistic dimension of sexual integrity and function, and that of immortality (narcissistic in nature) through fantasies of filiation and transmission would be prevalent. The primary narcissism of each partner and the narcissism of their "group reality" will extend in the necessary idealization of fantasized child, the common and shared conjugal narcissistic object.

However, the fragile narcissism of the two partners could be traumatized, wounded by the plan to interpose a child between their very fusional couple.

We shall also have to look into the lack of desire for a child in the couple at a later point.

Monique Bydlowski (2008) and Sylvie Faure-Pragier (1998)[37] have particularly explored the set of questions surrounding the desire for child, especially through their research on the different forms of sterility.

In *Les enfants du désir*, Bydlowski[38]considers that contemporary couples' desire for a child fits in with prospects for individual and conjugal fulfillment. It finds expression in the individual and common creative reveries, unconscious and conscious fantasized activities that we are studying within the framework of parenthood.

She considers that the desire for a child in young women results from the harmonious combination of three components: the desire for identification with their first love-object, the maternal primary object; the œdipal desire to replace her in relationship to her father and to obtain a child-gift from him; finally the desire to identify with a woman as a seductress and as a mother enabling her to have a fully adequate encounter of sexual love for an actual man.

She further points to another aspect to take into consideration. A woman would also be motivated by a "debt of existence" owed to the woman who gave her life, her mother, and that the child is literally going to incarnate. Thus, by engendering, and particularly through birth of the first child, women would therefore fulfill their "duty of gratitude" toward their own mothers, often giving to her their first child to raise for a time.

What about men? They are primarily concerned about the integrity of their narcissistically overinvested sexual potency and their need for reassurance. So, for them, the desire for a child and its conception will serve to protect them from their castration anxiety, reactivated within this context, and to consolidate their "narcissistic integrity." The œdipal significance is also obvious. Desiring a child means unconsciously desiring to become a father in the place of one's own father, something which reactivates the œdipal conflict and its burden of anxiety-provoking guilt. The desire for a child will also respond to the narcissistic desire for immortality attainable by the procreation and enrollment of the child in a symbolic lineage and filiation.

Finally, the desire for a child can reveal a man's feminine-maternal component, which will resonate harmoniously and potentially conflictingly with that of his companion.

In the above-mentioned book on the "babies of the unconscious," Faure-Pragier first makes a pertinent distinction between the contemporary appearance of a demand, of a "right to a child," and the individual desire for a child. In a number of women, the "demand," the "right," would reflect a concern not only to do what is normal, to conform to social expectations, but also a desire to be fully recognized as an adult and to fulfill a duty to her husband and her family. This connects up with the representations of traditional societies according to Françoise Héritier, while, as concerns the desire for a child, she observes the presence of a dissociation of two currents – the investment of female sexuality and the desire for a child – that develop in parallel fashion and overlap from time to time without mixing.

Is this not just a means, a "transformational object" (C. Bollas),[39] sought for to eliminate archaic suffering for which it is not the solution? Is it a matter of repairing "female castration," as Freud believed? Thus, Faure-Pragier explains, the child is not only desired for its own sake, but also as the bearer of a phallic quality. Through it, her patients try to identify with the image of the complete, perfectly fulfilled mother that they perceived their mother to be. It is maternal phallicity that they are seeking more than a male penis.[40] This is how she describes the narcissistic dimension of the desire for a child and its goal of narcissistic completeness as also finding expression in a woman's unconscious through the phallus in Grunberger's thought.

From the couple to the family: the birth of a child

An anthropological perspective

Maurice Godelier has found that, "*nowhere, in any society, do a man and a woman alone suffice to make a child. What they make together, in proportions that vary from society to society and with a diversity of substances (sperm, menstrual blood, fat, breath, etc.), is a foetus, but never a complete, viable human child.*"[41] Other agents more powerful than human beings – deceased persons, ancestors, spirits, deities – must intervene and cooperate with humans by adding what is lacking – a soul, a spirit, a generally invisible component – in order to transform the foetus into a child.

In addition, making:

> *ordinary* humans . . . in all societies normally supposes sexual relations, whatever role the society attributes to given male or female substance in this process. Of course, all societies accept the idea that certain children can be born without the woman having had sexual relations with another human being. These are exceptional births and they play a large role in the

82 Sketching a "natural" history of the couple

construction of these societies' politico-religious universe, but they are not daily occurrences, not the general rule.[42]

Moreover, all these collective representations of the process of making human children assume an essential social function, according to Godelier, that of inserting an unborn child into three types of relationships. Thus, it will take its place in a socio-cosmic order, becoming, for example, a child of Sila, the Inuit master of the universe, who will give it a soul and its breath. At the same time, the child will take its place in a social and moral order, meaning that from birth, it will belong to one or several kinship groups, depending on the principle regulating descent in its society and will maintain kinship ties with its diverse rules, rights and duties. Finally, by its sex, male or female, it will immediately be placed into a sexual order, therefore, into relations of superiority (even of domination) or inferiority (even of subordination) vis-à-vis individuals of the other sex.[43]

A sociological perspective

François de Singly[44] considers that, while continuing to contribute as an institution to the biological and social reproduction of society, today's family – enduring space of affective and personal relations based on love and trust – exercises another function that has become central in our individualistic society, that of constructing individualized identity, of discovering one's child self. Today's family is indeed responsible for producing "modern" individuals.

Contemporary mother and father roles

Going from an upbringing whose function was the moral shaping of the child to upbringing centered on self-discovery and personal fulfillment results in a modification of family relations as a whole. To be consistent with these new principles and objectives of child raising, fathers and mothers can no longer continue to play the classic roles: the woman as homemaker, lady of the house, already close to her children, teaching obedience and good manners, compensated by displays of affection; the father, provider of income and authority figure. Today, we particularly observe a breakdown in the paternal model characterized by a devaluation of the "obedience–authority" pair and concern to be close to one's child, the new challenge for modern fathers being knowing how to be close while acting as a mediator vis-à-vis the outside world and an agent of socialization vis-à-vis rules.

Men are assuming a "non-authoritarian" authority role, an integral part of their position, and are achieving this by actually being co-responsible with their companions. They do not have many privileged, *tête-à-tête* relationships with their children. Moreover, fathers differ from mothers as much by the nature of the time spent raising the children as by the objective length of time they spend parenting and above all by their relationship to time itself. Men in fact seek to compartmentalize spaces, to separate time – professional time, non-professional time/family, conjugal, personal time – by avoiding mixing things. They seek to preserve their personal life, which is not mixed with home life. François de Singly explains that professional time is perceived by many men as being a form of indirect parental time. Consequently, the father's professional work is an integral part of his role as a father and he remains the principal person responsible for his family's standard of living. A man's professional investments remain a priority and structure male identity more than female identity, and even more the identity of the man-father than the identity of the woman-mother. There is therefore a patent differentiation of genders. Moreover, a man invests in the family in a paradoxical way by setting objectives of personal success for himself that must have an impact on the family group. Therefore, a man's "family self," unlike that of the woman, is a self that is entitled to be a "personal self" at the same time. His family identity does not require his continuous presence.

Contrary to the father's time, the mother's is much less well-defined. Socially constructed and personally internalized, being a mother is by definition being available. This characteristic of a woman's time finds expression in the lack of boundaries, which even encroaches upon her professional work. For the woman, working *caring for others* tends to take up, at least in the home, all her time. It corresponds to her making herself available for her family. A mother's professional life, which is secondary, does not have the same identity significance as for men, the priority of which has already been underscored. Here we meet up again with Winnicott's idea that, unlike men, women are "continuous," contributing thus to conferring upon their child or children a continuous feeling of existence structuring their identity.

Psychoanalytic perspective

A traumatic event, the birth of a child disrupts the psychic functioning of the couple and its members, both dynamically and economically, with a reactivation of diverse conflicts, the anxiety and defenses correlative to them, displacements of flows of investment, a stimulation of unconscious, preconscious and conscious fantasized activity, as well as reshuffling of the interplay of identifications.

With regard to the reactivation of the two partners' œdipal issues, let me mention the possible or difficult identification with the œdipal father for the father, with the œdipal mother for the mother, with the incestuous fantasy of having created this child with and/or for the father, with and/or for the mother. To be noted is jealousy, sibling rivalry with the child, reactivation of each one's sibling complex, especially that of the father with a possible feeling of his exclusion by the mother.

To be taken into consideration as well is the possible existence of implicit or explicit envy on the part of the husband with regard to his wife's motherhood, reflecting his own reactivated female desires for motherhood.

Let me point to possible displacements, both of the partner's hostility toward the child in order to maintain a critical couple relationship and of a feeling of love and idealization directed toward the child fulfilling its father or mother, something which was no longer possible with the partner.

84 Sketching a "natural" history of the couple

Some questions necessarily arise, among them: What place is to be accorded to this child within the psychic space of each of the parents and within the conjugal psyche? Of what types of investments will it be the object? What representations will be formed of it, and accompanied by what affects? What identifications and projections will be at work? What functions and roles will the couple and each of the parents attribute to it?

How will the parenthood of the mother, of the father and of the parental couple be experienced and exercised? What unconscious alliances will be established between the parents and their child or children, and what will be the topographical, dynamic and economic repercussions within each party and within this new family space?

What about these new antagonistic relations between the couple in love, or conjugal couple, and the parental couple?

I have chosen to study the ideas of a certain number of specialists in order to try to contribute to finding answers to these questions. Thus, I shall look at the invaluable and complementary reflections of Catherine Parat, Michel Fain and Denise Braunschweig and, finally, those of Serge Lebovici and Leticia Solis-Ponton on the subject of parenthood.

CATHERINE PARAT "THE ŒDIPAL ORGANIZATION OF THE GENITAL STAGE" (1967)[45]

For Catherine Parat, œdipal organization is characterized by a dual relationship within a three-way system: a heterosexual relationship with the couple's heterosexual partner and a homosexual relationship with the "others" external to the couple to whom their child or children belongs or belong. From this perspective, the child will be the object of a dual parental investment, on the one hand, as "other" right from the beginning of its existence and, on the other hand, as an object investment that will evolve in parallel with the child's own development in order finally to meet up with the former. Having become independent, the child becomes an "other" and belongs to the world of "others."

Right from the beginning of its existence, the child is going to have twofold value for both the mother and the father:

- a direct value as an object, first narcissistic, for the mother especially, being part of her own body and invested as such, which is determinant for the constitution of the child's narcissism, then pregenital (oral, anal, phallic), because its demands and the needs expressed during the course of its development reverberate in the mother, and sometimes also in the father.
- a different value as an œdipal object in a relationship of love between a man and a woman, the child of a couple.

The evolution of these two original types of investment of the child is going to make possible the establishment of a relationship that will progressively make the child an other among the others, an other having the value of a third party in this trio of œdipal

Sketching a "natural" history of the couple   85

organization, something which will enable it to structure a genuine triangular possibility, then an œdipal organization. Children thus help maintain the triangular system and, in this way, contribute to the parental couple's œdipal equilibrium.

MICHEL FAIN AND DENISE BRAUNSCHWEIG

In *Eros et Antéros* (1971),[46] Michel Fain and Denise Braunschweig provide some indications concerning the differentiated nature of the roles and parental, maternal and paternal, investments in accordance with the child's sex.

According to them, there are two forces of nature: the maternal instinct, one of the aspects of female sexuality, and the father's desire to impose an œdipal structuring on the mother–child relationship as early as possible.

They note the concomitant appearance of the baby's auto-eroticism and of the revival of the sexual interest of the woman, who is its mother. Thus, this auto-eroticism identifies the baby with its ex-mother, who for a moment has become an erotic woman again, lover of the father-husband, which they call "censoring the lover in her." It appears as a pleasure combatting the disintegrating effects of maternal absence, as well as the child's excitation-screen system. It is uncovered in the sense of a withdrawal of a narcissistic cover provided by its mother.

Fain and Braunschweig explain that the mother of the child and the wife of the father are beings with scarcely anything in common. When the mother disinvests her child to turn to her man, it is not the latter that she reinvests first, but herself. She thus steals part of her child's narcissism to use as make-up.[47]

Generally, the mother, mediator of the paternal law and of phallic narcissism, covers the girl's and the boy's femininity, and "uncovers" the boy's virility. Indeed, she exercises all her power of repression, in its primary form, over her son's feminine tendencies, while the father is fundamentally ambivalent, fundamentally œdipal vis-à-vis his son, especially his oldest son. He will use his œdipal hatred to make his boy virile and do his utmost as soon as possible to condense the notion of transgression with the mnesic trace of the mother's inexpressible love for her first son.[48]

As for the daughter, projecting paternal narcissism on her must contribute to the constitution of her own female narcissism. Moreover, lacking a penis, she is led to invest, not the vagina, but her own body, as an object of love with a big share of auto-eroticism that comes to compensate for what she experiences as a narcissistic wound. The mother's imposition of reactive formations, among them cleanliness and disgust, will contribute to the development of the girl's concern about her appearance, which therefore includes the relatively late integration of an anal component, notions of "dirty" and of "ugly" taking the backseat.

Constructing parenthood

According to Leticia Solis-Ponton (2008),[49] the desire and plan to have a child launches the construction of parenthood as a psychic process that will be crystallized by the child's parentalization of its parents.

86 Sketching a "natural" history of the couple

For his part, Serge Lebovici (2002) maintains that parenthood is something completely different from biological kinship. To become a parent, he explains, it is necessary beforehand to have engaged in work on oneself that first of all consists in understanding that one inherits something from one's own parents,[50] which is a matter of intergenerational transmission and implies, therefore, also thinking about one's descendants, which is first of all about the imaginary child. I shall return to this later on. He furthermore considers that pregnancy stimulates the parents' primary narcissism, which will enable them to be good, happy parents, and to exercise their parenthood. He introduces the notions of transgenerational history, transgenerational mandate and tree of life, all mobilized in this vast domain of parenthood. For him, transgenerational history involves elements of the story of the parents' and grandparents' life, which often conflicts; but it also involves the mythical child. All these elements are going to be concentrated in the transgenerational mandate that is transmitted to the child,[51] who will therefore be the bearer of it and will later be able to modify it with its parents.

What about the representations of the baby in each parent's mind?

Synthesizing Lebovici's conceptions, Leticia Solis-Ponton discusses the construction of four representations relating to each parent's family and childhood history, to their multiple identifications, all the while knowing that, in reality, it is rather a matter of a composite elaboration. It is a matter of representations of the imaginary baby, the fantasized baby, the narcissistic baby and the baby of the culture.

The imaginary baby is the baby that the mother consciously and preconsciously imagines, heir to her desire for a child, elaborated since her childhood. During her pregnancy, Lebovici thinks, the mother imagines the child that she is going to give to her husband. The choice of a first name, the sex, plays an important role in this. Thus, the first name chosen will involve many things, sometimes difficult ones, such as a secret, a suicide, or a hero that the child unconsciously makes her think of, and the child will assume this whole legacy, which will play an important role in its future. That is why Lebovici maintains that the imaginary child is also the one who is the bearer of transgenerational history.

The fantasized baby is the bearer of the mother's unconscious fantasies, is often tied to conflicts relative to her œdipal issues. In the case of women who experienced a difficult childhood, this representation may be expressed by fears of malformation, even death, or of a hostile being who could prey on her from within. The narcissistic baby is the baby tied to maternal narcissism. Finally, the baby of the culture is the cultural representation that each woman possesses of motherhood and childhood, of ways of fitting the child into the kinship group, with its duties and its rights.

Upon being born, the real baby will trigger diverse affects in its mother and its father, and will inevitably be confronted with multiple representations of the "child within," which will mix together and alternate in the exchanges with the real baby, involving an imaginary, fantasized dimension. This birth therefore initiates a new family triad – animated by multiple (behavioral, affective, fantasized and symbolic) interactions, within which the baby will find a place determined in

Sketching a "natural" history of the couple 87

accordance with varied factors – but also the critical, "mutative" transition from the conjugal couple in love to the parental couple, in which the "processes of parentalization" effected by the child itself come into play.

Within this triad, the mother plays the dual conflictual role of mother and wife, and her presence will be divided up between baby and her husband, who will alternately become the third component of the founding triangle. Thus, she will be caught between her "primary maternal concern" and even beyond, and her "censoring the lover in her."

This primary adaptation of the mother to the baby's needs enables the creation of a dyad in which, contextualizing their exchanges, the father plays a role of third party. But, in the mother's head, this father is also a fantasized psychic presence incorporating the mother's father.

Leticia Solis-Ponton, moreover, thinks that "censoring the lover in her" introduces the child to the threefold difference of parenthood: the difference between Ego and non-Ego, that between the sexes, and that between generations. Finally, she considers that this transition from the conjugal couple to the parental couple constitutes a *natural transition* – since it takes place due to biology – and *early*, because even when the couple has engaged in planning the baby, the unfinished condition of the human being makes this transition into a trial: a *paradoxical* trial because of the elements of the unconscious life of the parents which are going to lead to regressive and progressive movements in order to reach, when all goes well, a more mature level of inter- and intrapsychic functioning.[52]

For my part, I shall look at the positive and negative repercussions of the structural conflictuality of these two couples – as lovers and as parents – in the following manner.

The parental couple and the family can destroy the couple in love. There is no longer any eroticizing of the relationship between the two partners, but only tenderness and a quasi-sibling and/or friendly relationship. This couple has become a parental team.

But the parental couple can also "be created" by the child who will keep it alive when it is in danger of breaking up because it is fragilized for diverse reasons. Each one's self-fulfillment can then be achieved through "fulfilling" motherhood and fatherhood while the love relationship is abandoned, because it is experienced as being too dangerous, invasive, even depersonalizing. By playing the role of separating-differentiating third party, the child will create a protective and life-saving distance between the two parents-lovers. Thus, the child and parenthood will be able to be idealized to the detriment of the conjugal love. Inversely, endangered by parenthood, the couple in love may attack the parental couple and the family leading to the abandonment of the child, experienced as an intrusion, a disruptive element. There is then no place for it in the enclosed conjugal space of the two partners. Its exclusion, the abusive mistreatment and lack of care of which it is the object, as well as the dearth of tender investment and the intensity of aggressive investments with regard to it can be tied to excessively symbiotic-fusional parental conjugal functioning, or threatened by its destructivity, as well as by œdipal guilt common

88 Sketching a "natural" history of the couple

to both parents subsequent to the "transgressive" creation of a child. Then, it is the one punished! It would be a matter of the reactivation of coordinated, resonating fantasies of the primal scene and fantasies of castration on the part of both partners, as well as the mobilization of processes of identifying with their child.

The childless couple, out of "free choice" or sterility

An anthropological perspective

As I have already said, in traditional societies, a childless couple as the free expression of an individual's and/or couple's desire is unimaginable. Remember that not transmitting life breaks a chain of which no one is the final link and, moreover, bars access to the status of ancestor. Thus, like marriage, procreation is a duty with regard to those who have gone before us in life.

In all places and at all times, sterility has been spontaneously understood in the feminine. It consequently insistently says something about the social relationship between the sexes, declares Françoise Héritier.[53] Indeed, sterility because of the man, independent of impotence, is not acknowledged. So, all the cases of conjugal infecundity are imputed to women and particularly to the ill will of their individual fate.

In traditional societies, it is not the loss of virginity, or marriage, or even motherhood that confers the status of woman upon a girl. It is conception. A pregnancy is all that is needed, and whether it is followed by miscarriage or birth is of little importance. Consequently, a sterile woman is not considered a true woman. It will be as if she had never lived in this world.

Héritier observes that the discourse on the causes of sterility, as well as the reasons for fecundity, express a natural homology between the world, the individual body and society, perceived, thus, as intimately linked, with the possibility of transfers from one of these levels to another. This homology manifests itself in variable symbolic contents, but in accordance with identical formal laws. Sterility is above all perceived as a social punishment, inscribed in the body, for acts that break the law, that deviate from the norm, and transgress strictly circumscribed limits. Three principal errors of conduct are penalized in this way: *crossing generations, crossing bloodlines, crossing genders,* when this is improperly and unexpectedly done.[54]

Psychoanalytic perspective

I shall distinguish between the couple that is childless by "free choice" and the couple obliged to forgo having children for essentially psychopathological and medical reasons. I shall then talk about the sterile couple and the multiple determinant factors involved.

The childless couple by "free choice"

How are we to understand this desire not to desire a child today in our individualistic Western society? For this choice predominantly concerns our society rooted in the omnipotence of the individual's desires, thoughts and actions, and in particular the desire for authenticity, self-fulfillment and control over one's personal life. Nevertheless, in their couple, contemporary individuals are also be subject to paradoxical injunctions that they owe it to one another to come to terms with: self-fulfillment/requirement of reciprocity; spontaneity/self-control; flexibility/self-consistency. These changes in values and normative models of thought and action are the correlates of a clear lightening of the burden of institutional constraints and of social morality, and therefore of the law and its symbolic structuring power, which finds itself being progressively transferred onto families, couples and individuals. In addition, I have amply discussed the multiple phenomena of dissociation or splitting, among them: procreation–sexuality; marriage or conjugality–sexuality; love–sexuality; erotic sexuality-discharge sexuality; erotic sexuality–hygienic sexuality; heterosexuality–conjugality. The sense of time has also changed and proceeds from this fragmentation. Time indeed seems fragmented and the subjects live at an accelerated pace, fixed in an ephemeral present, in quest of immediate pleasures, without past and without projection into a long-term future that is too anxiety-provoking.

All this suggests to me a prevalence of pregenital, narcissistic elements, of primary psychic processes, of an omnipotent pleasure principle combined with a lack of œdipal and genital elements, of secondary psychic processes, of sublimations and symbolizations that are thus evidence of functioning characterized by distinctly narcissistic and perverted aspects.

That is why, before inquiring into the existence of psychic determinants, I might advance the idea that the present-day choice of not desiring to have a child is symptomatic of our society and in a different manner confirms the fundamentally ambivalent nature of the desire to have a child.

This choice may be the man's or the woman's, or both. The choice expressed in an overt way by one partner, although the other might reject it, can also consciously represent a repressed, unconscious, negative desire. This reflects the couple's unconscious, intersubjective organization, where one of the two will perform a phoric function of spokesperson for the couple's lack of desire. An excessively symbiotico-fusional conjugal organization could view the child as a stranger, an intruder, a persecutor reactivating fantasies of persecution, but also a sibling complex that has not been worked out. From a group perspective, one might imagine the need to perpetuate a form of group illusion, which is therefore a state of conjugal omnipotence tied to a traumatic experience of exclusion from a persecutory primal scene.

Let us also look at the partners' and the couple's objects of investments that will not allow making room for a new, potentially disruptive, object. Their desire for self-fulfillment would not involve parenthood. Granted, but what about their respective œdipal issues and how they interconnect within their intersubjective organization? Identifying with the father and the mother in the primal scene, taking their place, would certainly present dangers to be avoided. The anxieties over castration and loss of love would then be reactivated and severely punished by the Superego. We shall not forget the hypothesis of eternally remaining the children loved by their parents, and therefore the desire to prolong childhood, without œdipal conflict or castration anxiety; similarly, the fear of identifying with violent parents, perpetrators of abusive treatment, and the vital need to spare in this way their possible children with whom they also identify. One may, moreover, encounter couples who have not overcome their œdipal conflict and, therefore, present major fixations leading, for example, to the woman identified with the œdipal little girl choosing a man representing a father figure who will bring her fulfillment. She will not be able to become a mother, and he will not want another child. The opposite situation is also conceivable. Another possibility is represented by a "sibling" couple in which each partner represents a narcissistic, bisexual double that is self-sufficient. The presence of a child would awaken violent movements of envy, rivalry and jealousy. Finally, what would underlie this choice of not desiring to have a child would also be a hostile, violent œdipal movement of rupture of filiation and the end of the bloodline.

The sterile couple

Sterility is defined as the failure to have a child after two years of sexual relations without contraception, surfacing, therefore, when this stops.

It often blocks the way to overcoming the œdipal conflict. The couple may experience feelings of failure, an awakening of persecution, depressive and castration anxieties. The two partners very often have a feeling of being kept indefinitely in a state of childhood and unjustly handicapped compared to others. At work may be: a hostile projection on the partner with the unconscious desire to frustrate her desire to be a mother, or his to be a father; self-punishing, masochistic forms of satisfaction tied to the fantasized realization of an incestuous desire; an unconscious conjugal desire not to have a child, because each partner could see him- or herself as a future bad parent; a feeling of œdipal guilt capable of keeping each parent from identifying with the parent of the same sex. Finally, from a transgenerational perspective, mourning in the family can prevent or inhibit procreation. In addition, shame, and some transgression to expiate through sterility, which would then wash away sins committed by ancestors, could lead to the extinction of the family line.

Let us distinguish between female sterility and male sterility, which I shall deal with, though succinctly, later on.

When a child is not forthcoming, medical examination looks for and often finds organic causes. Sylvie Faure-Pragier, who has particularly explored the field of female sterility, considers that, on the psychodynamic plane, it is important to treat all sterile women in the same manner, whether or not they suffer from organic damage, because they all present the same type of unconscious conflicts. So, rather than defining an illness, the concept of psychogenic sterility would designate a psychic dimension present in all sterility. She considers that when it comes to fecundity, the interweaving of the psychic and the physiological more typically appears to be the rule. The psyche in fact produces organic damage, which, inversely, has repercussions on the mental functioning. Sterility would thus introduce veritable circularity, where the influence of the psyche and the body on one another would be recursive. Consequently, it would be caused by the effect it produces. Body and psyche would auto-generate their anomalies.

She reminds us that sterility can be a matter of an œdipal conflict, as Freud proposed. The symptom functioning in a hystero-phobic manner, the child desired would be the child of the incestuous fantasy with the father, the œdipal child. But the fear of retaliation by the rival mother would come to hinder the realization of this desire for conception.

Nevertheless, Faure-Pragier has above all detected the existence of a powerful counter-investment of hostility toward the persecuting, intrusive, all-powerful mother imago. To account for this psychic dimension present in all sterility, she has introduced the concept of "inconception" as the psychic side of this biological reality that is sterility having depression as its model. What is its content?

It is a matter, she maintains, of patients presenting "character neuroses," organized defensively with regard to a depressive nucleus. The narcissistic suffering is not felt consciously, but is the object of a denial of the psychic functioning as a whole, also, and particularly, concerning femininity and what are considered to be its characteristic components, such as passivity, dependence and receptivity. She observes the prevalence of a pathological bond of dependence and submission to a mother experienced as phallic and omnipotent, which she explains by an insufficient attachment to the father, discredited by the mother, leading to a denial of the paternal role and above all of the love between the parents, of maternal femininity, thus producing a failure of "censoring the lover in her." This is why the unconceivable baby would not be the father's œdipal child, but the mother's baby, begotten for the mother, or that the mother begets for the daughter, often with the conscious project of satisfying her or of narcissistically restoring her, whence comes the fantasy of begetting a child homosexually, from mother to daughter. Indeed, it seems to Faure-Pragier that unconscious homosexuality appears to play a dominant role in sterility, primary homosexuality, repressed in its passive aspects, which should enable any daughter to leave behind her primary identification in order to evolve toward post-œdipal, secondary identifications, her father especially.

Faure-Pragier has also detected in these women the absence of narcissistic investment of the reproductive system, as well as a sexual investment in general, probably in connection with a lack of investment on the part of the mother of these capacities in her daughter. Thus, marked by passivity, receptivity and the capacity to contain are generally consciously rejected for that reason, without the consequences of this rejection of her fecundity becoming apparent to the woman.

What about penis envy and the desire to have a child in these sterile patients? In these women, penis envy appears rather to be a defense, a solution to an excessively fusional relationship with the mother, leading to a phallic identification as a late means of separation. It is therefore a matter of a counter-identification with the mother. Passivity, femininity with regard to the mother, representing an intolerable

92 Sketching a "natural" history of the couple

threat because too destructive, would consequently make phallicity seem a better solution, and infecundity would, thus, be an expression of unwillingness to be submissive to the mother. Planning to have a child may then express homosexual love, or violent hostility toward the mother, feelings that are often associated with one another. It would be the daughter who begets the child for her mother, or the mother who begets the child for her daughter. Consequently, it does not seem, either, that the request expresses a genuine desire for a child born out of the love of a man and a woman. Faure-Pragier suggests that one might perhaps speak of longing for a child, which may mask unconscious, complete refusal to have one.[55] Indeed, she maintains that the desire to have a child may hide the refusal to have a child. This imaginary child may be a "killer," an infantile part projected from the powerless passive self or, yet again, it would be the projection of the woman's mother herself.

Couple specialists need to think about how this type of psychic functioning on the part of a sterile woman connects with that of her partner to produce conjugal sterility. In other words, in what way or ways would the man's functioning potentialize or, on the contrary, be able to inhibit, that of his partner, and vice versa? Would female sterility be enough to produce conjugal sterility without the unconscious participation of the woman's partner and vice versa, and in what ways? An intersubjective interpretation of sterility especially endeavoring to explore the unconscious benefits that this sterility procures for each of the partners would need to be developed. The notion of "symptom-bearer" would be pertinent here. Moreover, a different interpretation, a group interpretation, would also need to be taken into consideration, revealing the nature and flow of conjugal fantasies giving rise to diverse anxieties, as well as the couple's structuring imagos, sometimes omnipotent, terrifying, arousing feelings of guilt, infantilizing, determining the conditions of future sterility.

As for male sterility, for a man, the lack of a child is, according to Monique Bydlowski, a source of psychic insecurity because there is no longer anything providing evidence of his narcissistic completeness with regard to his lineage. Thus, male infertility would express itself rather as a reflection of filiation, a series of hypotheses on the man's place in his lineage and in the world. Male infertility would thus differ from female infertility in terms of impact.

Growing old together

This new critical trial imposed by the reality of aging is going to determine necessary and inevitable changes in each of the partners and within their couple. So, let us ask where things will stand with the mourning of the loss of their own bodily youth, of their ideals, of realized and unrealized dreams of desire. What will become of the reciprocal investment of the other person's body, and of conjugal seduction and its new means of expression and satisfaction? How will the investments with regard to the partner and the couple be reorganized? What will each one's and the couple's sublimating capacities be? Finally, what topographical, dynamic and economic changes will be at work, both on the level of the intersubjective relationship

Sketching a "natural" history of the couple 93

and on the group level, and what would their processes be? How will their "work couple" evolve and what will become of their socio-cultural reality?

With Gerard Le Gouès (2000)[56] and Henri Danon-Boileau (2000),[57] let us tackle certain aspects and changes connected with aging that will help better identify the essential issues facing the aging couple. For this purpose, I shall take a look at the characteristics of psychic aging, sexuality, the critical stage of retirement and grandparenthood.

Certain characteristics of psychic aging

According to Le Gouès, the beginning of aging may be situated in middle age in connection with the mid-life crisis and the arrival on the psychic scene of our "ineluctable finitude" imposed by the prospect of death, which triggers a major existential crisis. Accepting our finitude is the fruit of a work of mourning by and upon oneself, as well as of the capacity to recognize narcissistic aspirations to eternity as being perishable. He distinguishes several stages: the aging adult, from middle age to retirement age; the aged subject, from the beginning of retirement to the age of 80; and the elderly person over 80 years old.

Aging is reflected in the losses and advantages that every subject must combine and handle:

- Losses wound one's narcissism, reactivating the problems surrounding castration that every subject has and that are conducive to reworking the depressive position. They mobilize the subject's defenses, which will help it protect its threatened inner world. These are those having diverse objects and functions, the most sensitive of which are reduced sexual potency in the case of men and decreased seductiveness in the case of women. The growing gap between desire and the means of satisfying it in fact reactivates the castration complex. Finally, I would like to mention the loss of self that determines necessary work of mourning of one's self and one's ideals. It is accompanied by an attack on our narcissistic integrity, in its aspects of omnipotence and immortality. For this mourning of oneself to succeed, at least up to a certain point, the good internal object must prevail over the bad; Eros must be stronger than the destructive drives.
- The advantages involve maturity, self-preservation, but also the capacity to enjoy living in different ways.

On the metapsychological plane, Le Gouès sees aging as a process establishing tension between the Ego and the Id. Indeed, the psychic apparatus would enter into a "conflict of finitude," a topographical conflict between the Ego that knows it is going to die, at least partially acknowledging its aging, and the Id ensconced in timelessness and the narcissistic fantasy of eternity that is unaware of it. The conflict would therefore play out reciprocally on the backdrop of a kind of reality test, starting from the degree of acknowledgment of finitude and of the desire for eternity.

For him, under normal circumstances, the structure of the psychic apparatus practically does not undergo change before the age of 80. He notes a decline in the Id's drive-impulse, an easing of the strictures of the Superego, less often mobilized to combat less lively conflicts. For its part, the Ego undergoes two major deformations in aging: weakening, mental expression of the lowered drive, determining diverse reactions such as mourning, depression, sublimations, multiple defenses; and the rigidifying that finds expression in the tendency to conform corresponding to the desire to oppose change, therefore, what is new, the unknown.

On the economic plane, the psychic apparatus undergoes two major modifications: the progressive lowering of the drive-impulse and fewer means of gratifying it. In the search for an economic, dynamic equilibrium between pleasure and "unpleasure," losses and what remains, advantages, sublimation as a solution, as a source of substitute pleasure, would represent, according to Le Gouès, the best means the psyche has to fight against the wounding, disorganizing effects of those losses. Unfortunately, sublimation is neither inexhaustible, nor accessible to all subjects.

The Ego's successful aging would, therefore, consist in accepting the loss of youth and the fear of death, of giving up and disinvesting objects, earlier goals, ideals, thus freeing energy that has become available to invest new ones adapted to its new situation. "Aging well" depends on the existence of a good sublimating game, on the aptitude to work out a castration complex jeopardized by late crises, on the capacity to make genital, bodily sexuality evolve into loving tenderness.

However, the aging subject's "neurotic" Ego rebels, refuses to engage in the necessary work of mourning and tries to resexualize its drives, possibly finding expression in the "noonday demon" in a man, the late desire to have a child in a woman, but also in pathological regression in the form of a defensive return of anality or orality during which these partial drives are more acted upon than sublimated. The "Borderline" Ego can find another means, such as that of defensive overcompensation through hyperactivity, grandiose plans, regaining its youth, evidence of a denial of its painful reality. It can also turn toward the body in the form of hypochondria. Finally, the "psychotic" Ego may develop in the form of resexualization, a late flowering, such as an erotic delusion, or in the form of anxiety-producing persecution, a delusion of being harmed giving free rein to projection.

The sexuality of aging subjects

In the vast majority of cases, elderly couples appear to adapt to their sexual aging, Henri Danon-Boileau observes.[58] In fact, with age, and depending upon their habits, sexual relations have progressively become less frequent. Sometimes, they end up disappearing, but one may find that, much more often than one might expect, sexual relations continue of which "nothing" would have given the slightest hint.

Psychic life remains one of desiring, producer of fantasized scenarios, up to the end, and object desire is what persists the longest. Aging insidiously separates the body from the psyche. So it is that bodily sexuality weakens first, before psychosexuality, and this temporal gap creates a space within the Ego attacking narcissism.

Le Gouès differentiates several forms of sexuality:

- Organ sexuality, corresponding to bodily sexual activity.
- Functional sexuality, corresponding to modes of sexual performance in keeping with the subject's psychic structure. He considers that late sexual difficulties are far more dependent on psychopathology than on physiology, provided that the aging individual remains free of severe organic illness. He proposes then to re-examine sexuality disorders in light of the conflictuality. As concerns impotence, especially, changes occur with age, and castration anxiety can accelerate functional castration. So, it would be desirable to develop the capacity to let things happen more slowly and more incompletely, to give priority to tenderness over performance, and accord greater importance to passivity–receptivity.
  Masturbation can act as a pathological refuge in elderly couples when sexual relations no longer exist because of the man's impotence, or because "we're too old for that" on the part of the woman, but it is particularly poorly accepted by the elderly, representing for them a pathetic act.
- Finally, "mentalized" sexuality is that which is dramatized in conscious daydreams and in night-time dreams.

In the aging couple, when the change of sexual level is sustained by good genital tenderness, the transition to re-adapted exchanges is not excessively damaging. Tenderness in fact represents the late solution to object-oriented eroticism.

Depending on what psychosexuality – oral and anal, in particular – is the most invested; the subject is going to cope with aging by trying to satisfy his/her hope of enjoyment. Anality plays a central role as soon as there is a drop in the libido, because aggressiveness is likely to come back and rapidly gain the upper hand. Thus, elderly people whose anality resurfaces quickly become mean as soon as they fall in love. But anality is also the living reservoir of partial drives that feed sublimation. As for oral sexuality, it activates the desire to eat in order to fight against the anxiety of absence, running the risk of late obesity and alcoholism.

The critical, wound-inducing stage of retirement

Retirees and elderly people who remain active live much longer and remain in better condition than other people do.

Let us recall, with Danon-Boileau, certain painful losses experienced at the time of retirement. To begin with, retirement marks an abrupt break with a part of what one is, the attack against one's own socio-professional, statutory identity. Hence, the feeling of self, of one's continuity, of one's self-congruence would, more or less, be challenged from the outside. It is also characterized by the quantity of free time, often experienced as emptiness, an anxiety-provoking mass of dead time and boredom. Within this anxiogenic and depressogenic context, the loss of one's usual social network, financial loss, loss of a job in which one has often invested a great deal and which has been gratifying in many ways, all pile up. And yet, the retiree feels that he or she is the same today as before. In other words, his or her resources, energy, could find a field, or fields, of application for overcoming the rupture, even if that requires significant conscious and unconscious readjustments. It is from this perspective of maintaining one's earlier equilibrium and psychic economy that sublimation will play a major, priority role.

Retirement, therefore, forces one to find a new equilibrium, a reorganization of sublimating possibilities, depending on the loss sustained. And, among the set of conscious and unconscious significations of overall professional life, one aspect or another of what seems lost (content, skill, power . . .), more or less easy to compensate for or replace by sublimations will prevail, depending on each individual. Women would seem to be less affected by depression. They know how to alternate practical life and family life, distractions and intellectual work much better than men do. Men see things in a more rigid and less diversified manner. The transition to sublimating activity is often facilitated by an extra- or paraprofessional interest preceding retirement. This investment prior to the inevitable wound would attenuate the feeling of rupture and discontinuity.

This stage of retirement is also critical for conjugal life, generating conflicts fed by hostile projective movements directed toward one's partner. If the two partners both find themselves in this new, potentially threatening, situation, therefore tête-à-tête, they will have to mobilize their creative and sublimating capacities in order to reconfigure their inner world and rearrange their couple's psychic economy and dynamic, especially by arranging and creating personal, as well as common and shared, objects of investment, times, spaces procuring them direct, libidinal, narcissistic satisfactions, aim-inhibited and sublimated ones in particular.

Grandparenthood

Henri Danon-Boileau also invites us to reflect upon grandparenthood and comes up with some "wise precautions" for elderly people.

He considers that the grandparental position "behind the front lines" involves an imperative duty to show discretion. Elderly people need to reflect carefully about the necessary amount of support, practical assistance, to give, as well as the amount of tact to be displayed vis-à-vis the new parents. Everyone knows that grandparents – unless they are "reasonably" called upon, or in an emergency – should not intervene in their grandchildren's upbringing and should avoid any intrusive or authoritarian behavior. Even the desire to win a grandchild's love should be controlled to a certain degree.[59]

From the age of 2 to 20 years or more, the relationship will inevitably undergo transformation. It will be the grandparents' job to know how to adapt themselves to the evolution of their grandchildren as their needs change, as well as to classic rebellious behavior, which does not, however, have anything to do with parent–child conflicts. Remaining just as available, just as indulgent, and just as loving, whatever use the young people will make of that in the course of their development, will provide grandparents with a feeling of security. They then "rediscover" their youth and enjoy their grandchildren more than they did their own children. Their power and self-esteem often having been damaged, they regain a feeling of power through the child's dependence and the quality of its regard for them.

Another aspect to be considered in this relationship between grandparents and their grandchildren is the fantasies connected with having "descendants," the elderly subject's identification with those who survive him or her. All the ideas surrounding the bloodline, continuity, children pursuing a personal project, would represent a defense against anxiety in face of the major renunciation demanded by death, passing away. Thus, perpetuating one's existence would shift from the subject to his or her filiation, another subtle solution to the narcissistic desire for immortality.

What about the impact of this grandparenthood on conjugal functioning and organization? Within the framework of the multiple losses and renunciations imposed by aging, grandparenthood would procure enormous benefits, individual as well as conjugal, narcissistic and objectal, creating and recreating various libidinal ties in the service of family conjugal and personal psychic life. It would offer another means of satisfying the narcissistic fantasy of immortality. In addition, it would enrich the grandparents' identity repertory, acquiring a new status associated with new narcissisizing functions, which will reduce the flow of hostile and conflictual movements within elderly couples made fragile on all levels. We could formulate the hypothesis that grandparenthood also represents a "countergift" from the children, a way of repairing, of restoring the wounded narcissistic integrity of their aging parents, therefore, of taking care of them, and of keeping their parental couple alive, the very one that gave them life, something which reflects Monique Bydlowski's idea of "debt of life."[60]

Notes

1 A. Girard (1964), *Le choix du conjoint, une enquête psychosociologique en France.* Travaux et documents de l'INED. Paris: Presses universitaires de France, 2nd edition, 1974. Michel Bozon and François Héran (1987), "La découverte du conjoint. Evolution et morphologie des scènes de rencontre." *Population*, no. 6, pp. 943–86.
2 *Op. cit.*, Kaufmann, p. 26.
3 *Op. cit.*, Bozon and Héran.
4 *Op. cit.*, Kaufmann, pp. 27–8.
5 Jacques André (1995), *Aux origines féminines de la sexualité.* Paris: Presses universitaires de France, 2004.
6 *Op. cit.*, David.
7 Jean-Georges Lemaire (1979), *Le couple, sa vie, sa mort.* Paris: Payot.
8 *Op. cit.*, Klein, "Love, guilt and reparation."
9 *Op. cit.*, Bouvet.
10 *Op. cit.*, Kaës, *Le complexe fraternel.*
11 *Op. cit.*, Kaës, *Les alliances inconscientes.*
12 René Kaës (1989), "Le Pacte dénégatif. Eléments pour une métapsychologie des ensembles transsubjectifs," in A. Missenard and G. Rosolato (eds), *Figures et modalités du négatif.* Paris: Dunod. pp. 101–36.
13 *Op. cit.*, Grunberger.

14 *Op. cit.*, Anzieu.
15 Donald Woods Winnicott (1971), "Creativity and its origins," in *op. cit.*, Winnicott, *Playing and Reality*, pp. 65–85.
16 *Op. cit.*, Ruffiot.
17 *Op. cit.*, Kaës, *Un singulier pluriel.*
18 *Op. cit.*, Lemaire, *Le Couple, sa vie, sa mort.*
19 *Op. cit.*, Kaufmann, p. 88.
20 *Op. cit.*, Grunberger.
21 *Ibid.*, p. 111.
22 Dona Francescato (1992), *Quando l'amore finisce*. Bologna: Il Mulino.
23 *Op. cit.*, Kaufmann, p. 118.
24 *Op. cit.*, Héritier, p. 112.
25 To begin with, William H. Masters and Virginia E. Johnson (1966), *Human Sexual Response*. Toronto: Bantam Books, 1981.
26 *Op. cit.*, Bozon, p. 76.
27 Michel Fain and Denise Braunschweig (1971), *Eros and Antéros, Réflexions psychanalytiques sur la sexualité*. Paris: Payot.
28 Jacqueline Schaeffer (1997), *Le refus du féminin*. Paris: Presses universitaires de France, 2008. English translation: *The Universal Refusal: A Psychoanalytic Exploration of the Feminine Sphere and its Repudiation*. London: Karnac, 2011.
29 Jacqueline Schaeffer (2002), "Le parcours des antagonismes entre féminin et maternel," in Leticia Solis-Ponton (ed.), *La parentalité, Défi pour le troisième millénaire*. Paris: Presses universitaires de France. pp. 139–57.
30 Jacqueline Schaeffer (2007), "D'une possible co-création du masculin et du féminin?" in Patrick de Neuter and Danielle Bastien (eds), *Clinique du couple*. Ramonville-Saint-Agne: ERES, 2007.
31 *Op. cit.*, Schaeffer. *Le refus du féminin*, p. 26.
32 Sylvie Faure-Pragier (1998), *Les bébés de l'inconscient, Le psychanalyste face aux stérilités féminines aujourd'hui*. Paris: Presses universitaires de France.
33 Sigmund Freud (1924b), *The Dissolution of the Oedipus Complex. S.E.* 19 London: Hogarth.
34 *Op. cit.*, Freud (1925), *Some Psychical Consequences on the Anatomical Distinction between the Sexes.*
35 *Op. cit.*, Freud (1931), *Female sexuality.*
36 *Op. cit.*, Freud (1933), *Femininity.*
37 *Op. cit.*, Faure-Pragier.
38 Monique Bydlowski (2008), *Les enfants du désir*. Paris: Odile Jacob.
39 Christopher Bollas (1989), *Forces of Destiny: Psychoanalysis and the Human Idiom*. London: Free Association Books.
40 *Ibid.*, p. 108.
41 *Op. cit.*, Godelier, p. 325.
42 *Ibid.*, p. 304.
43 *Ibid.*, pp. 312–13.
44 François de Singly (2004), *Le soi, le couple et la famille*. Paris: Nathan.
45 *Op. cit.*, Parat.
46 *Op. cit.*, Fain and Braunschweig.
47 *Ibid.*, p. 39.
48 *Ibid.*, pp. 36–7.
49 Leticia Solis-Ponton (2008), "Le passage du couple conjugal au couple parental: un parcours semé de mines interpersonelles," in *Dialogue*. Toulouse: Eres. pp. 19–30.
50 Serge Lebovici (2002), "Entretien de L. Solis-Ponton avec Serge Lebovici," in Leticia Solis-Ponton (ed.), *La parentalité*. Paris: Presses universitaires de France, p. 10.

51 *Ibid.*, p. 11.
52 *Op. cit.*, Solis-Ponton, "Le passage du couple conjugal," pp. 25–6.
53 *Op. cit.*, Héritier, p. 89.
54 *Ibid.*, p. 130.
55 *Op. cit.*, Faure-Pragier, p. 111.
56 Gérard Le Gouès (2000), *L'âge et le principe de plaisir: introduction à la clinique tardive.* Paris: Dunod.
57 Henri Danon-Boileau (2000), *De la vieillesse à la mort.* Paris: Hachette.
58 *Ibid.*, p. 55.
59 *Ibid.*, p. 195.
60 Monique Bydlowski (1997), *La dette de vie: Itinéraire psychanalytique de la maternité.* Paris: Presses universitaires de France.

Chapter 5

The concept of *couple work*

A necessary introduction to the concept of *couple work*

Having come to the conclusion that there is a "natural history" of the couple, of its critical, mutative and maturing stages, and diverse levels of existence studied from a pluridisciplinary perspective, I should now be able to provide a unified, pertinent account of all those psychic, socio-cultural and historical factors determining the life of the couple and its durability despite its fragility and vicissitudes.

It was with surprising clarity that the interdisciplinary concept of *couple work* suddenly came to me as something that could help to interpret conjugal facts pertaining to each of the three realities – sexual-bodily, psychic and socio-cultural, each endowed with their own temporality – as well as understanding both their necessary interconnections and shortcomings. Indeed, while *couple work* is sufficient and satisfying for certain couples, it also enables us to envisage failures – that is to say, shortcomings, excesses, unbalances – among the three realities, especially displayed in varied forms of suffering that can lead to conjugal breakup or to consulting a specialist, a couple therapist, for example.

So, the time has come to inquire into the diverse aspects and characteristics of this work as a function of those engaging in it – its areas of activities, the processes at work and its productions. It is also necessary to reflect upon its functions and the objectives the two partners expect to attain. Moreover, its varied failures will lead us to explore and discover certain obstacles, inhibiting – even paralyzing because they are too exhilarating – agents, as well as, paradoxically, to think about facilitating and stimulating factors.

Allow me to point out that this is a matter of a working hypothesis whose operative and heuristic value must obviously be evaluated, through discussion and, especially, through comparison with clinical and socio-anthropological material.

Presentation of *couple work*

I see this couple work *as being realized conjointly by each partner's Ego, invested to a greater or lesser extent, on three levels: unconscious, preconscious and conscious. It involves economic, dynamic and topographical aspects, and would therefore be accomplished within the three realities of the couple already described (psychic, sexual-bodily and socio-cultural), the temporality of each one of them conditioning the corresponding work.*

Within psychic reality

Let us recall the three levels: group, intersubjective and intrapsychic-individual.

The group level

A *conjugal group* exists when a common, shared psychic construction occurs between the partners, a "conjugal psyche" that will function as such from then on and will, in particular, produce "conjugal compromise formations," themselves common and shared. It therefore results from work to synergize and conflictualize the parts of every individual psyche mobilized to construct this conjugal group. Thus, each partner will be divided between the need to abandon part of his or her identifications, thoughts and ideals in order to maintain the group and his or her ties with the group, on the one hand, and the requirement to maintain his or her own psychic space, on the other.

Along with Kaës,[1] mention might be made of sets of processes, organizers and modes of "synergism" of these parts of individual psyches. Among the four sets of processes identified, let me cite: originary, primary, secondary and tertiary processes; projective and introjective, adhesive identifications; mechanisms of projection, of deposits with defense mechanisms; phoric functions.

To be associated with these sets of processes are organizers, such as fantasies, imagos, as well as unconscious alliances, which I shall discuss later on.

In addition, there is the primordial participation of the objectalizing function (in André Green's sense)[2] of the love-object and of this conjugal group as a manifestation of the partners' Eros conditioning even this work.

Moreover, in conjunction with Kaës' ideas,[3] one may mention the existence of two principal poles – isomorphic and homeomorphic – that structure the relationships between each partner and the conjugal group. Indeed, this "conjunction" is set in a state of tension between the similarity and the difference between the psychic spaces, underpinned by depersonalization anxiety. This conjugal group must, therefore, necessarily organize itself in accordance with modalities where what is common and what is shared prevail over what is private and different. As a conjugal group, or dyad, there will be a joint narcissistic investment of the boundaries separating it, delimiting it and protecting it from the "world of others," from third parties (parents, children, friends, other people) in various different ways, the object of *couple work*, which will also regulate the types of relationships established with them. Jürg Willi has observed that, depending on the couple, these boundaries need to be "unclear," "clearly-defined, but permeable" or "fixed." He advocates establishing boundaries that are clearly drawn with respect to people on the outside, the couple's parents and children, which is one of the goals of all

102 The concept of *couple work*

therapy. He has, moreover, given thought to the role of third parties in certain situations where the couple find experiences.[4] Catherine Parat reminds us that, taking the place of the third person in the œdipal structuring, this extra-conjugal world receives a complex investment of a homosexual nature from each of the partners in contrast to their reciprocal heterosexual investment. Indeed, the affects making it up are to a small extent non-sublimated, and to a large extent sublimated.[5]

Finally, this *conjugal group* is also endowed with a "fantasized, common and shared living body," the place where its psyche dwells. For Anzieu,[6] in the imaginary activity of both partners, this bodily metaphor refers to the mother's womb and the fœto-maternal relationship. Does not one say, or does not one hear it said, that "everything is fine *in* our couple" or, on the contrary, "things aren't going well, there's no space to breathe, it's stifling, it's confining . . ."? The couple is, indeed, fantasized by both its members not only as a "womb-like living body," but also invested as a living, growing being that has functional and psychic vital needs to satisfy and will inevitably go through mutative and maturing critical periods: it breathes or must breathe; it must be nurtured or someone must nuture it (by contributions from the outside and from within); it must move, go into action, evolve, mature. Inspired by what Winnicott has written about infants,[7] I would say that, as a nascent group, the couple is animated by an innate creative drive conferring upon it creative potentialities in connection with the illusion and that it is endowed with an innate potential for growth, integration and maturation. It must make its inner energies circulate, but also eliminate waste, noxious, undesirable elements, and, notably, project them upon third parties. Finally, it thinks, plans, communicates and fantasizes, and the conjugal psychic reality is, therefore, found, located in this "fantasized living body" primordial to it.

I believe that the self-preservation drives will be at work within this *fantasized living being* that they will animate. Nevertheless, this representation of living being, of "womb-like living body" different in each of the two members, will awaken, or be able to awaken, varied fantasies generating diverse, essentially archaic, anxieties of being devoured, of persecution, anxieties of a depressive nature, for example.

Intersubjectivity

The *intersubjective space* animated by a multi-faceted conflictuality connects each partner's object-relations, realizes an interplay of identifications and projections contributing to the creation of unconscious alliances, and establishes a reciprocal relationship between the two partners' Œdipus and sibling complexes.

It is to be emphasized that Bouvet[8] considered that an object-relation was both objectal and narcissistic, therefore receiving a twofold investment drive, while Grunberger argued for pregenitality with a dialectic dynamism setting orality and anality against one another. So it is that the oral relation is characterized by a subject/object confusion, and the anal relation is a typical subject-/object-relation, a social relation *par excellence*. An anal component would be present in every objectal relation because it is at the energizing roots of that relation.

The concept of *couple work*   103

In keeping with Grunberger's insights,[9] I could put forward the idea that an anal component is always active in every psychic construction of a couple. Moreover, necessary antagonic and synergetic participation of the oral and anal components would be at work in varied doses:

- Through subject/object confusion, the oral object-relation would be mobilized on the group level, that of narcissistic union, of the "couple fantasy."
- Through organization of conjugal life and "work couple," the anal object-relation would prevail on the level of intersubjectivity, which is conflictual.

Finally, with Benno Rosenberg,[10] the distance between the desiring Ego and its object will depend on the more or less pronounced participation of the death drive, which will also come into play in the possibility of differentiating the object, of nuancing it, contributing to enriching the objectal relation. Consequently, according to this line of thought, the death drive would come into play in the differentiation of psychic spaces and at the homeomorphic pole defined by Kaës.[11]

Rosenberg, moreover, has shed light on the role of masochism, as guardian of the life of the couple and a factor in its durability. So, a good interplay of the entangling–disentangling of drives between Eros and destructive drives would condition the necessary joint work of masochism in the service of the life of the couple. This durability of the conjugal relationship is also determined by the "work of the death drive" at work, according to Green,[12] in inhibiting the aim of the sexual drive, especially finding expression in the flow of tenderness.

As for unconscious alliances, they are those of the realization of desires, but also those of structuring, defensive, even offensive ones for certain couples, at least during certain periods of their lives. Among the structuring alliances, I may mention along with Kaës,[13] the mutual secondary narcissistic contract consisting in according oneself a place in the couple provided that this contributes to its continuity and preservation. It is comparable to a contract of affiliation with a group. However, this contract is transformed during the fundamental crises of the couple's existence, during mourning and separations. Another mutual contract active within the couple, and also requiring repression, is that of the mutual renunciation of the direct realization of destructive instinctual aims.

Before turning to a discussion of the individual level, how do things stand with flows of instinctual investments and topographical aspects on the group and intersubjective levels?

Drawing inspiration from Winnicott[14] and Grunberger,[15] I identify an organization within couples involving two poles:

- One, which I call narcissistic, is the "conjugal group," a conflictual, omnipotent, site of massive narcissistic investments, "pure female" according to Winnicott, based on the Ego/love-object identity, "narcissistic union," generating the feeling of a "conjugal Self," narcissistic agency and reserve of energy, different from the "conjugal Ego," in contact with socio-cultural reality and animating the "work couple." Common formations of the "conjugal Superego" and of the "conjugal Ego Ideal" will co-exist in a state of dynamic tension with the "conjugal Self" and the "conjugal Ego."

- The other objectal, intersubjective, conflictual, place of erotic, tender and aggressive, narcissistic investments; "pure male," based on the instinctual objectal relation, separate Ego/love-object; the whole constituting the "couple's psychic bisexuality."

The conjugal group, fantasized living being and shared common creation, though differentiated in each of the partners, then seems to represent a third psychic object within the intersubjective love relationship, which therefore proves to be triangular, something which would suggest the existence of an œdipal structuring of every conjugal relationship that would then take part in the consolidation of the partners' œdipal equilibrium. Moreover, this third object can be imagined as being the "psychic cradle" or "maternal womb" of the future child to be born.

Kaës has introduced the concept of "intersubjectivity work." He considers that intersubjectivity imposes psychic work upon the psyche by the very fact of the subject's necessary intersubjective situation and that the intersubjectivity work would be the psychic work of other person's unconscious in the subject's psyche. This is naturally the case, but he necessarily integrates the identification work and its transforming repercussions on the partners' Egos.[16] This psychoanalytic notion is to be compared with "conjugal socialization work," a concept proposed by the sociologist François de Singly to designate the set of processes of transformation of the individual within conjugal relations, especially those connected with each one's identity components.[17]

The intrapsychic-individual level

This space is also animated by multiple anxiety-generating conflicts and correlative defensive measures that each partner will have to attempt to resolve in order to accept entering into the conjugal relationship and co-creating the conjugal group. These occur between Ego and object, identity and alterity, self-preservation and sexuality, narcissism and objectality, pregenitality and genitality, male and female, Eros and destructive drives, between their love-object and couple-object or "couple fantasy" (individual representation of the conjugal group), as well as between each one's shareable and unshareable objects. It is also helpful to remember the importance of each one's psychic bisexuality work. As Jacques André has emphasized, the very fact of entering into a conjugal relationship revives the originary situation of "primitive femininity" and would constitute one of its primordial conditions.[18] How? By connecting the traumatic, breaking-in dimension through the mutual intrapsychic penetration of the seductive and seducing object with the necessary movement of drive openness and passivation.

Let us once again examine with André Green[19] the conflictual situation that each one's Ego experiences in itself. It is caught, on the one hand, between the

The concept of *couple work*   105

compulsion to synthesize, particularly at the origin of narcissism, and, owing to its dependence on the Id, the desire to be but one with the object, on the other hand.

While the love-object, for example, is the goal of the satisfactions of the Id, for the Ego, it is always in certain respects a cause of unbalance, a "trauma." While the Ego aspires to unification extending to unification with the object, this total reuniting obliges it to lose its organization with the danger of depersonalization. And when this is impossible, it disorganizes the Ego, because it does not tolerate this separation. Thus, the Ego is the seat of the trauma and of the reactions to the dependency on the object, unknown, so variable and changing, incontrollable, and yet so necessary. It wounds the Ego's narcissism and its desire for mastery, equivalent to the re-establishment of its integrity.

Let us finally consider the multiple anxieties triggered by these different sectors of the couple's reality. We shall in particular find those that are pregenital, schizoid (splitting up the body and the psyche), persecutory, depressive, those involving intrusion-separation in the Ego's relationship with the love-object, œdipal (castration). Certain of them will predominate at certain levels and will mobilize corresponding defenses.

Within the socio-cultural reality

In the socio-cultural reality, the conjugal couple in love must necessarily also constitute a "work couple," which will supply it with the material means of its social existence, positioning it in the vast, complex, stratified, differentiated social structure.

Thus, *couple work* will involve work in the home, conjugal socialization work, parental work (when the conjugal couple becomes a parental couple), among other forms of work fitting into the more general framework of work for the development of a conjugal culture and identity made possible by the preliminary work accomplished within the psychic reality.

Referring back to the ideas of Bion and Anzieu about groups, this "work couple" or "technical pole" (in Anzieu) therefore corresponds to one of two levels of conjugal functioning. The other level would be the fantasized couple in interrelationship with it, which will nourish it with fantasies and drive investments, but also limit it by means of anxieties and defensive measures. It therefore represents a form of voluntary, conscious cooperation between the two partners in the accomplishment of different common tasks in relationship with the couple's material and social existence. For Bion and Anzieu, it would involve the Ego's characteristics, here the "conjugal Ego" governed by the reality principle and animated by the logic of the functioning of the secondary psychic processes. This cooperation is obviously not exclusively rational, "secondarized," but also permeated, even disturbed, by a paralyzing or stimulating, conscious and unconscious, fantasized and emotional flow. Thus, born of a conjugal reality, the convergence of the two partners' fantasies and their unifying elaboration would lead to compromise formations, such as ideologies, mythologies, utopias (in Anzieu) that will orient and determine the general representations of conjugal life, the daily activities and plans, just as they

106 The concept of *couple work*

will have an impact on the different types of work realized and, finally, on the elaboration of a conjugal culture and identity.

Indeed, living together assumes the creation of common, shared space-times that will inevitably stand in a tense relationship with the partners' separate and differentiated space-times. It is a matter of fields of fantasized fomentation and flow, of multiple symbolizations and sublimations, within which individual and conjugal compromise formations will be worked out, finding expression in: the creation and investment of activities that are common and shared, as well as differentiated and separated (professional, extra-professional, leisure activities); the elaboration of common and unshared representations and ideas (those of the man and of the woman, of their respective roles in the couple, of their relationships within the couple, those of the couple, inspired by their respective families, those of the family, in particular); the establishment of stable and variable forms of communication, of norms of conduct, of rules of domestic organization and functioning – mobilizing both partners' anality – of common ideals and values, of mythical tales, of ritual activities evolving into habits, among which sexuality also figures; the establishment of institutions said to be conjugal.

One can also envisage the organization of a conjugal economy involving income, budget, expenditures and modes of consumption, and savings investment behavior. The distribution of power, the modes of exercising it and its differentiated sectors would also be something to take into consideration. Then, there are the modes of investment and the conscious and unconscious representations of their habitat, "the couple's bodily envelope," the interplay of investments between their couple, sphere of intimacy, its boundaries and the external world, the relationships between private couple/public couple and a possible split between them. Finally, the investment of shared and unshared time, and their individual and common temporality (past, present, future), are also significant sectors of conjugal life.

Let me emphasize that within these different sectors, sociologists fairly regularly detect manifestations of a difference between the sexes: in domestic work and parenting; in the professional investment structuring the male-paternal identity more than the female-maternal identity; in the investment of the couple where women would play the role of "guardian"; in the forms of communication; in the exchanges of "goods and services" and the complexity of their flow reflecting both partners' differentiated expectations; in the relationship to sexuality, above all, after the birth of children, therefore, during the "mutative" transition from the conjugal couple to the parental couple; in conflicts, for example.

What about the nature of energy employed by this *couple work*? Is it a matter of sublimated libido, essentially of anality, of which we know it represents the principal reservoir? Would it also be a matter of what is called the actual energy of each of the partners' self-preservation drives, pooled in the service of the life and preservation of the couple?

Topographically, the "conjugal Ego" at work in the "work couple" is nourished by sublimated aggressive, erotic and narcissistic energy, as well as what is called the actual energy of self-preservation drives. It establishes varied dynamic relationships

The concept of *couple work* 107

with extra-conjugal reality and the couple's other psychic agencies: the "Superego," restraining and prohibiting; the Ego's Ideal, prescriber of norms of conduct, of values and of ideals, of common projects, in particular; and, finally, the "conjugal Self," a narcissistic structure.

Within the sexual-bodily reality

It seems to me that on the level of bodily reality, *couple work* consists in: investing and maintaining narcissistic, erotic, tender and aggressive investments of the other person's body; constructing representations of separate sexual bodies, and a "fantasy of psycho-bodily pairing"; identifying with the other person, mobilizing one's own psychic bisexuality for that; communicating narcissistic, erotic, tender, aggressive messages in diverse ways, for example, verbally and non-verbally, behaviorally, mimetic-gesturally, all of them finding expression, in particular, in a capacity to be concerned about the other person's body, to be seduced by his or her body, to seduce it with one's own body and also to reject it as if an alarm bell has gone off.

A question arises about the fate of "psychosomatic organizations" in the course of conjugal life. Would they be better protected from disorganizing trauma when *couple work* is satisfactory, meaning when it can act as an excitation-screen?

On the contrary, would the bodily repercussions of *couple work* be potentially pernicious, because it is traumatogenic, and therefore disorganizing – thus expressing the failure of this work? Reflection upon a "couple psychosomatics" needs to be undertaken, inquiring in particular into the role of the couple and *couple work*, through its diverse modes of participation in the psychosomatic economy of the partners. Inversely, one might inquire into the repercussions of somatic disorganization experienced by one of the members on the three levels of conjugal reality, something needing to be expanded upon at a later stage of research.

Diversified in its repertory of practices, the couple's sexuality procures aggressive, erotic (pregenital and genital), narcissistic satisfactions. In heterosexual couples, the two libidinal currents – heterosexual and homosexual – will be able to be satisfied, directly in the first case, and, in the second, through fantasizing by identification with the partner. Its investment will vary as a function of the conjugal culture, the stages of the conjugal cycle, the evolution of each of the partners and of the economy of its investments, the evolution of certain aspects of their intersubjective relationship, in particular. It will be able to achieve a certain balance with each one's auto-erotic sexuality.

Psychoanalytic discourse discusses the realization of a state of narcissistic completeness (Grunberger),[20] reassurance about its narcissistic integrity (Green),[21] the acquisition of a feeling of psychic security, experiencing oneself as "good" (Klein),[22] as well as the realization of the fantasy of an "imaginary common body," fantasy of bisexuality denying the difference between the sexes, castration and alterity. However, it also emphasizes the necessary underlying psychic work, individual work (Schaeffer's "female work," for example)[23] combining with that of the partner mobilizing the difference between the sexes, each

108 The concept of *couple work*

one's bisexuality, multiple identifications, coping with pregenital and genital anxieties, the specific conflicts between the erotic dimension – with the retentive nature of desire, and that of instinctual discharge – as well as between sexuality and the narcissistic desire not to differentiate and, finally, between sexuality and self-preservation.

The necessarily different discourse of sociologists sheds light on some aspects of *couple work* on this level. Thus, Michel Bozon[24] points out that the functions of sexuality differ depending on the phase of the conjugal cycle. In the early phase, sexual activity contributes to the very construction of the couple as an intersubjective relationship and group reality, while, owing to men's professional investment and women's investment in motherhood, it becomes less central at the phase called stabilization. It becomes a "habit for holding the couple together," a "private ritual that symbolically and periodically reaffirms the couple's existence."[25] For his part, François de Singly deems that the work of "conjugal socialization" would also come into play in the mutual recognition of the sexual component of the partners' identity.[26]

In sexual-bodily temporality, there is an inevitable discrepancy between the psychic and socio-cultural temporalities, which is a source of conflicts and anxiety, above all, as the partners age. *Couple work* endeavors to solve them through adjustments and better connections between the three realities making up the couple.

Reflections on the purposes, antagonisms and repercussions on the partners in *couple work*

Realized conjointly by the partners' Ego, this *couple work* must be able to conflictualize and realize economic, dynamic and flexible connections among the three realities, thus ensuring tolerable, durable and satisfactory conjugal functioning, both for the couple and for its members. Nevertheless, it is inconceivable apart from in its structural, therefore, ongoing, antagonism with each partner's individual work ("work of the individual"). So, over the course of time, how will each one's Ego distribute its investments between individual work and *couple work*? In other words, what portions will it be able to devote to itself and to the couple? Moreover, inevitable differences will spring up between the two partners with respect to this antagonism, as well as regarding the preferential investment of one conjugal reality or another, differences which will or will not be compensated for by the partner's work. These differences will probably vary during the course of the conjugal cycle, but will also be able to appear fixed, something which runs the risk of causing conjugal difficulties.

Before taking up the question of failures of *couple work*, let us ask about its impact upon each partner's psychic organization and functioning, meaning upon the topographical, economic and dynamic aspects.

What would be potentially positive about it? Would it have structuring or reorganizing, narcissisizing, excitation-screening, protective, reassuring, stabilizing virtues, stimulating on the level of activities of representation and enriching

The concept of *couple work* 109

for the individual Ego? What would be potentially detrimental about it? Could it present dangers of disorganization, of depersonalization of the Ego, an attack on its narcissistic integrity? Does it have economically traumatogenic potential conditioning the later development of evolving or reversible somatic forms of disorganization? Are there aspects of it that are too anxiogenic, destabilizing, inhibiting and impoverishing for the Ego and, finally, aspects that are disentangling and reactivating narcissistic wounds?

Lastly, if one understands each partner's conjugal life as the expression of the necessary dynamic interconnection between *couple work* and individual work, each having its respective share combining with the effects of the partner's *couple work*, would it rather be beneficial for certain people and detrimental for others? The answer is also tied to the existence of possible failures of *couple work*. What would they then be?

The failures of *couple work*

There are diverse ways of conceiving these failures. Quantitatively speaking, one may point to insufficient Ego work on the part of both parties, or on the part of one of the two, which is not compensated for by the other's work. They may concern one or several realities, the result being experienced as unsatisfactory by one or both partners, potentially conflictual with hostile projective movements, which will lead to conjugal suffering.

What do I mean by going to excesses when it comes to *couple work*? We can understand this as an exorbitant investment in this work on the part of the Ego of one or both of the partners to the detriment of individual work, something which will have harmful individual repercussions at a later point with consequences for the couple. This can, furthermore, be a matter of the over-investment of one or several realities to the detriment of others, making this economically costly with potentially disorganizing effects owing to later impairment of the work.

Qualitatively speaking, one may point to aspects that are systematic, fixed and therefore not very flexible and unable to be mobilized, not creative enough – modalities of accomplishing *couple work* independently of the realities (sexual-bodily, psychic or socio-cultural).

I shall also look at work to establish connections between these three realities, work that may be insufficient or excessive, as well as work providing consistency and harmonization among the temporalities proper to each.

If one of the major functions of *couple work* is to ensure a certain durability to conjugal life, apart from any form of suffering (psychic, social, sexual-bodily), one of its failures would lie in insufficient good masochism mobilized by both partners, in the poor quality of the flow of tenderness deriving from aim-inhibition of the sexual drive, in difficulty using the weak sublimated homosexual undercurrent within the heterosexual relationship, producing a kind of friendship between the two partners, as well as the inability of mutual narcissistic contributions to enable each one to regain a certain narcissistic integrity within the couple.

110 The concept of *couple work*

This *couple work* and its failures inevitably gives rise to questions about the notions of normality and pathology in the couples' lives together, about its functions, its evolution over the course of individual and conjugal time.

Normality and pathology in couples' lives together

Couple work, which is carried out within the three realities – psychic, socio-cultural and sexual-bodily, each with its own temporality, and its diverse and varied failures – enables us to forgo a discussion in terms of the normality/pathology of individuals and couples, and to consider that conjugal life – initiated by a mutual choice made by both partners determined in accordance with multiple modalities – proceeds from genuine differentiated, comprehensive work unfolding within a complex temporality and taking its place in a relationship of conflictuality with each partner's individual work. So, no matter what each one's pathological dispositions may be, the construction, then the functioning of a couple, therefore, presupposes this joint work, which may temporarily or durably fail over the course of time on one or several levels of reality with various sorts of repercussions on the other levels.

The causalities will also be multiple. Consequently, even if *couple work* produces individual and/or conjugal symptoms within the psychic reality, one will not be able to speak of couple pathology, especially if the symptoms procure benefits for both partners. However, if their impact on the other levels of realities – socio-cultural (the reality outside the couple) and sexual-bodily reality – is pernicious, one will have to bring up the existence of failures of this work manifesting themselves in different signs causing possible conflicts in these areas of suffering and having necessarily negative consequences upon the couple's psychic reality.

"Couple pathologies" do not therefore signify either the absence of couple psychic work, or the steady presence of suffering, but rather the production of psychic functioning that will possibly have negative repercussions on the other levels of conjugal reality ultimately leading one to speak of the failure of this work. The same is true of failures on the level of socio-cultural reality or of sexual-bodily reality that will have negative consequences on the conjugal psyche.

Some functions of *couple work*

Let us not forget that within each conjugal partner's Ego, this *couple work*, joint work, is constantly in a state of tension with what is called individual work.

Some functions correspond to each of the three levels of its reality.

Psychic functions

Besides its functions of providing the members of a couple with very regressive direct narcissistic satisfactions – symbiotic and fusional aspirations – as well as with fantasized satisfactions through male and female identifications made possible by

The concept of *couple work* III

the mobilization of each partner's bisexuality, *couple work* also responds to protective, defensive needs vis-à-vis internal dangers (pregenital drives, homosexuality, destructive drives, multiple pregenital and œdipal fantasies and anxieties) and external dangers (projected conflictual or persecutory objects) that are satisfied by making unconscious defensive alliances (denegative pacts). Moreover, in subjects with a fragile social, psychic organization, it would make it possible to provide a "framework," a structuring function, suggesting to me the function of the "auxiliary Ego" of a mother for her infant.

Triangulation ensured within the intersubjective love relationship by the co-creation of the *conjugal group*, common and shared *fantasized living being* and "psychic cradle of the future child to be born" contribute to the consolidation of the partners' œdipal organization.

Finally, I want to mention the couple's repairing function, particularly highlighted by the work of Vincent Garcia (2007). Among the regressive and transferential movements at work favored by the partners within this "space" that is the couple, he has in fact detected repetitions of early traumatic experiences awaiting psychic "inscription" that will ultimately be elaborated, symbolized and consequently be "treated" in view of being "repaired" by and in the couple – whence comes the fundamental importance of the choice of partner. The couple therefore seems to him to be this space within which the archaic traumas – understood as situated somewhere prior to the mnesic trace – will be able to go back to work, to be revived.[27]

Sexual-bodily functions

Apart from the protection of the psychosomatic organization and the durable two-fold investment – narcissistic and erotic – of his or her own body and that of the other person, reciprocally, there are the direct erotic, tender, aggressive, pregenital and genital, heterosexual satisfactions and the homosexual ones, fantasized through identification with the partner. The strengthening of conjugal identity and that of the sexual component of the identity of each of the partners is also to be associated with this.[28]

Socio-cultural functions

As I have already explained, the couple and its work must ensure its material and social existence, produce the means to achieve that and satisfy its needs in this conjugal domain. It must create a conjugal culture conferring a singular identity upon the couple. I again especially speak about work in the home, work of conjugal socialization. When the couple becomes a parental couple, it must engage in parental and family work – child raising, for example.

Finally, *couple work* must conflictualize these three levels by establishing dynamic liaisons and economically balanced investments of a libidinal and self-preserving nature.

Notes

1 *Op. cit.*, Kaës, *Un singulier pluriel.*
2 *Op. cit.*, Green, *The Chains of Eros.*
3 *Op. cit.*, Kaës. *Un singulier pluriel.*
4 Jürg Willi (1975). *La relation de couple.* Paris: Delachaux & Niestlé, 1982.
5 *Op. cit.*, Parat.
6 *Op. cit.*, Anzieu.
7 *Op. cit.*, Winnicott. *The Maturational Processes.*
8 *Op. cit.*, Bouvet.
9 *Op. cit.*, Grunberger.
10 *Op. cit.*, Rosenberg.
11 *Op. cit.*, Kaës, *Un singulier pluriel.*
12 *Op. cit.*, Green, *Life Narcissism, Death Narcissism.*
13 *Op. cit.*, Kaës, *Les alliances inconscientes.*
14 *Op. cit.*, Winnicott, *Playing and Reality.*
15 *Op. cit.*, Grunberger.
16 *Op. cit.*, Kaës, *Un singulier pluriel.*
17 *Op. cit.*, de Singly.
18 *Op. cit.*, André.
19 *Op. cit.*, Green, *Life Narcissism, Death Narcissism.*
20 *Op. cit.*, Grunberger.
21 *Op. cit.*, Green, *The Chains of Eros.*
22 *Op. cit.*, Klein "Love, guilt and reparation."
23 *Op. cit.*, Schaeffer. "D'une possible co-création du masculin et du féminin?"
24 *Op. cit.*, Bozon.
25 *Ibid.*, p. 54.
26 *Op. cit.*, de Singly.
27 Vincent Garcia (2007), "Le couple: un lieu pour se réparer?," in Serge Arpin (ed.), *Le divan familial, Rencontres entre Familles et Culture.* Paris: Les Editions In Press, pp. 89–102.
28 *Op. cit.*, de Singly.

Chapter 6

The suffering couple, their request for consultation and the psychoanalytical work

Circumstances of the first consultation

For several years, I have seen the number of couples coming to consult me about different types of suffering increasing. Indeed, through the intervention of the mass media informing people of the existence of various forms of help for couples (counselling for couples, therapies, consultation with doctors, general practitioners, gynecologists, sexologists and psychiatrists), they are coming for consultation at a younger and younger age and earlier and earlier in their life as a couple, often upon the initiative of the woman.

The principal reasons for this are various feelings of dissatisfaction, critical, personal and conjugal stages – some of which are potentially mutative and maturing – and conflictualities exacerbated by these critical periods and events.

Let us take a closer look at the following situations.

- *The relationship between the two partners is experienced as being inadequate.* For example, their communication is felt to be inadequate, difficult, even blocked and they seem to suffer from this. They no longer understand one another and as soon as they begin speaking to one another, they end up arguing. Let us ask whether this symptomatic compromise is not a way of creating necessary distance between them, protected in this way owing to this inadequacy, from feared, latent, symbiotico-fusional aspirations (Lemaire, 1998).[1] Indeed, not communicating, not understanding one another, arguing, is also a way of limiting the density of potentially dangerous, depersonalizing relationships.

  On the level of erotic life, it may be not only a matter of a loss of desire and of any form of seduction, but also of certain forms of suffering. Indeed, certain forms of sexual dysfunction (frigidity, impotency, premature ejaculation, dyspareunia), often presented as being due to one of the partners, represent another form of setting limits on the density of the relationship and its fusional risks experienced within a satisfactory sexual union.

- *The other frequent situation comes from conflicts between partners.* The conflict can be understood as a symptom, a compromise formation (Lemaire, 1979),[2] a mutual reaction of narcissistic, identity affirmation serving the self-preservation of each person and finding expression in hostile reactions. Among certain of its effects, let us note that of reinforcing the insufficient individual boundaries of each partner. Furthermore, in my view, it is a "noisy" expression of the fundamental antagonisms between Ego/object, identity/alterity, narcissism/object-relations and that of the difference between the genders.

- *Correlative crisis of the transition from the conjugal couple to the parental couple, from the couple to the family.*
- *Physical and/or psychic conjugal violence,* which will raise questions for us regarding their transferential/inter-transferential significance and their fantasy dimension or dimension of pure discharge of excitation without any representative content.
- *Extraconjugal affairs or "extraconjugal acting" on the part of one partner*: factor of crisis and/or critical symptom?

   Different incidents may arise in the life of the couple, in the man and/or in the woman. We shall most certainly look for the existence of over-determination.
- *The existence of a symptom in one of the partners troubling conjugal functioning.* We may cite depression and other psychopathological troubles, problems with conduct (alcohol, drug use), a more or less serious bodily illness.
- *The presence of a symptom in a child of the family.* One may discover that this symptom manifested by the child is tied to a problem the parental couple has. Thus, hostile reactions can be displaced from the parental couple to the child, protecting their idealization and avoiding the expression of unbearable ambivalence. The noisy pathology of an adolescent may sometimes be understood as a means of bringing about treatment for the parents.

   It may also be a matter of a conflictual relationship in a new couple within a reconstituted family.

   But these couples may also come to consult me in order to undertake "separation work" that will be to the benefit of both partners and enable them to attenuate the inevitable suffering inflicted, not without guilt, upon the children they may have.

These consultations, early or not, attest not only to a failure of *couple work* but also to a more pronounced contemporary concern accorded to the quality of conjugal life, as well as expectations for and demands made on it, something unprecedented up until now in Western history.

However, these painful conjugal situations, which a number of couples find unmanageable, have become factors threatening to break up the couple, something that must raise questions for us.

The three preliminary interviews

Characteristics of the analytical consultation with a couple

The analytical consultation is eminently phobogenic for both the patients and the analyst, which explains, on one hand, that couples come for consultation relatively infrequently given the extent and duration of their suffering and, on the other hand, that there are not very many analysts who work in this area.

The consultation, or session, is, to begin with, a *transitional* space-time during which the two partners meet together and can meet together, talk, talk to one another, listen to one another, listen to themselves, take the time to listen to the other person and to listen to themselves, even be obliged listen to the other person, in the presence of a third party, the analyst, something which reduces the explosive, conflictual intensity of their dual confrontation in everyday life.

This analytic situation, within which each one's words acquire new substance, value, even meaning, is both *doubly asymmetrical and doubly triangulated*.

This third-party analyst is consciously perceived as being a referee, a mediator. He or she is in fact quickly invested by each partner and by the couple as a transferential mother figure, available, receptive, containing his or her patient-children's suffering, placed in a sibling relationship, reviving then the œdipal version of each partner's sibling complex. But the analyst is also invested as a protective Superego figure, setting limits fairly, as well as being a critic, prohibitor, observer and guardian of the consultation setup. That is an initial form of asymmetry and triangulation.

However, this analytic situation exposes the analyst to the regressive investment of a position of "parentified" child before a flawed parental couple in difficulty, reviving a sadomasochistic, exhibitionistic or tender "primal scene," as well as satisfying his infantile voyeuristic desires. His or her aloneness before the parental couple, who maintain solidarity with one another, creates another form of asymmetry, all the more so because its traumatic impact is great.

This situation, although anxiety-producing, is fundamentally reassuring, renarcissicizing, individuating and subjectivizing for each one of the partners, restorative for the conjugal group, but also relibidinalizing and relinking for the intersubjective relationship. While talking and feeling listened to procures narcissistic benefits, the couple can also experience feelings of failure, reactivating depressive and castration anxieties, anxiety about the incapacity to cope with their problems alone. They often experience more or less conscious feelings of guilt and shame, being obliged to give up their privacy before a stranger, parental figure and object of a resistance reinforcing the ambivalence of their present undertaking.

Moreover, coming as a pair brings with it the danger of talking about oneself and the other person in his or her presence. It is a matter of unveiling one's psychic universe, therefore, of a potential weakening of one's system of protection. For certain people, this danger of finding out what the other person is going to say or not say about him- or herself, about the other person, about the couple, may be great. It may also be dangerous to verbalize thoughts, emotions and fantasies to one's partner outside this neutral, protected space. That is why it is preferable and more reassuring to do it there. One of the risks would be the perverse use of what is said and heard as procuring a weapon for a future domestic conflict. From that point on, that place will be invested with ambivalence.

As I have already indicated, sibling rivalry is re-enacted within this doubly triangulated regressive space where both partners would be seeking attention, exclusive love and narcissistic support from the parental figure represented by the analyst.

This may take the form of "phallic" competition, with the desire to be the most seductive when it comes to verbalization, expressing emotions and fantasies and the quest for satisfaction of fantasized expectations of the therapist. The couple may also seduce through suffering and engage in rivalry when it comes to its degree and mode of expression. This brings me to mention the desire of the victim, designated by the couple, to be protected from his or her partner-aggressor by the analyst and to induce in him or her a masochistic identification movement as well as a counter-transferential feeling of rejection and hostility toward the partner-aggressor. One may observe a process that begins with masochistic seduction, then evolves into a perverse manipulation of the analyst causing an unconscious alliance between the victim and the therapist. This transferential movement informs one about the unconscious aspects of the conjugal bond and about the partners' repressed infantile emotions.

Analysts must accept being used as object, being manipulated to a certain degree, something which will enable them, through their analysis of the counter-transference, to understand certain unconscious aspects of the couple's functioning.

The necessary identification movements with each of the partners, male and female, call upon the analyst's bisexuality, which requires difficult psychic gymnastics.

Finally, let us take a look at this analytic situation constitutive of a "therapeutic group" with its dynamic and its specific psychic economy, which will produce a form of "group psychic apparatus," one of the agents of the evolution of the analytic process.

Thus, this particularly ambivalent and phobogenic situation produces multiple transferential movements determining a complex, composite counter-transference which I shall explain at a later point.

A complex interplay of alliances will have to be updated within this transfero-counter-transferential, homosexual and heterosexual, father–daughter, father–son, mother–daughter, mother–son, brother–brother, brother–sister, sister–sister dynamic.

The exploration of different areas of conjugal life

During the three preliminary interviews customarily fixed, I proceed with a general exploration of the consulting couple, of their objects of suffering and of their request, which will enable me to propose joint psychoanalytical work or other therapeutic help more adapted to their current situation.

Symptomatic exploration

This will concern present and/or past symptoms, complaints, reproaches, conflicts, (present and/or past) mutual expectations, as well as the articulation of complaints

The suffering couple 117

and grievances of the one with respect to the other. I systematically envision the existence of a multifold definition – individual, intersubjective and group – of a symptom discussed. Thus, what does a partner feel with regard to the symptom of his or her partner and what does he or she imagine? What function(s) do they perform within the couple and what unconscious meaning(s) are to be attributed to this?

Exploration of the present functioning of the couple and of certain aspects of its evolution

I inquire into some principles of functioning, certain distributions of roles within the organization of the household, their references to parental couples, the modalities of exchanges, of communication, both verbal and non-verbal. In addition, I show interest in the conditions of the founding and structuring of the couple, as well as in certain stages of its evolution, critical stages, in particular. Finally, I ask each one of the partners to introduce him- or herself individually, to discuss his or her life story and their family context.

Exploration of the individual requests and of the group request

The psychotherapeutic request assumes that the partners are ready to move from the level of complaining, of the symptoms, to that of their meaning or of their different meanings, with the intention of taking an active part in changing them and changing the couple, to calling it into question, with the risk of reactivating old conflicts, mourning and wounds. Nevertheless, this request is fundamentally ambivalent, attesting to unconscious forms of resistance to change correlative to latent benefits drawn from suffering, therefore to be uncovered. Moreover, the one who is suffering or is complaining is not necessarily the one who formulates the request. The other person will perhaps be the spokesperson for this within the framework of the intersubjective arrangement. But each person can also interactively oppose the other person's therapeutic project. In a group transferential process, in the course of which the couple invests in an infantile regressive position, the couple may expect to have decisions made for them by the kindly analyst-parent, who will have to point out this transferential reaction to them and bring them to reflect upon it, something which will have notable dynamic effects. The analyst must adopt a neutral, non-pressuring attitude toward the decisions made and especially raise questions of psychodynamic value about divergences in points of view, about feelings of reticence, as well as affirmations that are too strenuous, lacking in nuance and about the urgency of treatment.

Exploration of the first transferential and counter-transferential expressions

As I have already mentioned, this initial exploration is important, but nonetheless complex. In fact, essentially characterized by the intensity of its intersubjective transferential or inter-transferential manifestations constitutive of the conjugal relation, the couple is also the source of multiple individual and group movements directed toward the analyst and the ambiance of his or her office, in particular. Those coming from the conjugal group are oriented toward the analyst in order to merge him or her into the "therapeutic group" formed by the analyst and the couple.

Consequently, *the counter-transference of the analyst, space of reception of the transference of each of the partners, inter-transferential movements and conjugal transference, but also tool of investigation and interpretation of these latter transferential movements*, will also be composite and complicated. Moreover, each of the partners, invested as a person, as well as the couple, will arouse counter-transferential reactions in the analyst that are to be differentiated from his or her counter-transference, which implies the investment of their psychic functioning.

Let me add that analysts' training, their theoretical positions, the school of psychoanalysis to which they belong, with its implicit or explicit ideology, have considerable influence on the way in which each patient will be listened to, and therefore received, constituting, then, an anticipated manifestation of his or her counter-transferential aptitudes and determining a basic counter-attitude orienting and selecting the reception of multiple transferential materials.

At the end of my exploratory interviews, I have enough necessary elements available to me to enable me to set down indications for therapeutic work with the consulting couple.

Indications and contra-indications

The indication, just as, moreover, the limits of the therapeutic possibilities, depends on the exploration of the couple as well as the characteristics of the analyst – his or her personal analysis, psychic capacities, training, experience and interests in certain conjugal problems, counter-transference in particular.

That is why good indications seem to be more inherent to certain characteristics of the analyst who would feel at ease, or more at ease, with certain types of conjugal dysfunction, as well as being exposed to certain individual and conjugal transfero-counter-transferential aspects, which would confer on him or her the feeling of being capable of helping and accomplishing "good work" with these couples.

Then again, in patients, I shall mention the verbalization, the reciprocal investment of the partner's psychical functioning and of the conjugal reality, as well as the two partners' capacity to engage in self-analysis.

I consider that the multiple forms of insufficient and conflictual communication, even communication that has become complex, as well as lack of input and conjugal narcissistic wounds accompanied by reciprocal hostile movements, represent some good initial indications. Nevertheless, the evolution always remains uncertain. Suffering in their erotic life (absence or temporary or lasting loss of desire, impotence and premature ejaculation in the man, frigidity and dyspareunia in the woman) remain difficult and their evolution unpredictable.

The suffering couple 119

Are there really contra-indications for therapy with couples?

Outside of rare situations like jealous delirium within the context of passional psychosis, melancolic delirium essentially dependent on the partner's attitude and those situations able to exacerbate the perverse and pathogenic effects upon one of the members, there are situations in which therapy would rather have more drawbacks than advantages, and could even aggravate, even temporarily, pathogenic effects, not to mention, of course, the analyst's overall feeling of discomfort and inability to be able to help certain couples

Presentation and establishment of the framework

A few rules

It is at the end of the third preliminary interview, once the analyst has proposed joint psychoanalytical work to the suffering consulting couple, that he or she will present the framework for the therapy, meaning the working conditions without which no therapy would be possible.

It is important to state clearly a few rules and help the couple to understand them. These conditions will thus make it possible to spot and analyze any possible subsequent attack on the framework.

A first rule concerns practical indications concerning the work sessions: imperative presence of both partners of the couple at each session, the absence of one of them therefore making it impossible; length (an hour); the frequency of the sessions (preferably weekly, if not, bimonthly); fixing the time and stating the fees for the sessions.

A second rule is the right and not the obligation to say what one thinks, what one feels and what one imagines, without being interrupted by one's partner – the same goes for thoughts, feelings, fantasies, memories, dreams at night – which is evidence of the therapeutic concern to make sure that the individual discourse goes smoothly, to solicit the activity of representation of each person and of the couple, as well as protecting the inner spaces of each person and his or her personal secrets. Thus, any transgression can be the object of questioning having dynamic value.

A third rule is abstention on the part of the analyst, which signifies that his or her relationship to the conjugal group and to each of its members will have to remain only on a symbolic level, excluding, consequently, any form of seduction and of intervention in the couple's real life, in the form of personal advice and of opinions in particular. "Here, one says things; one does not act on them. We are here to understand and to analyze what occurs or what has occurred, and not to make decisions that you will make together elsewhere."

Technical aspects of the psychoanalytical work

Dealing with the three levels of their psychic reality (group, intersubjective and individual), this psychoanalytical work with couples is a space-time intermediary

120 The suffering couple

between their suffering, corresponding to a failure of their *couple work*, and, on the one hand, the discovery of their conjugal functioning – but also of each partner's psychic functioning – and, on the other hand, the advent of positive changes made possible by obtaining the means conducive to the realization of much more satisfactory *couple work*, the impact of which will be favorable to sexual-bodily and socio-cultural realities.

The preliminary work, nevertheless concomitant with the interpretative activity

While the strategy is based on the interpretation of the multiple individual, conjugal and, above all, inter-transferential movements, through the counter-transference of the analyst, it necessarily involves some fundamental conditions and tactical aspects. Let us take a look at them.

According to Béla Grunberger (1971),[3] *respect and restoration of the patients' narcissism* are fundamental elements of the analytic process, just as the analytic situation organizes a veritable "narcissistic union" between the patient and his or her analyst which it is important to respect because its therapeutic potential is so great. And the analyst's silence contributes to creating this union comparable to narcissism of sleep.

So, I must *be attentive and respect, as well as quite often restore, each partner's narcissism and promote the narcissistic reinvestment of the conjugal group, wounded, experienced as a "bad object" by each one*. How? In particular, *through the twofold "well-tempered" use of silence, not only on the part of the analyst, but also on the part of the conjugal partner who must listen without interrupting the speaker*. Silence is in the service of the progress of the transferential investments, on the one hand, and of the interpretation on the other hand. Consequently, it is in the service of the analytic process.

In doing so, the "therapeutic group" will function as a "narcissistic union" making it possible to create a "group illusion"[4] ("we work well together; we are a good group; our analyst is good") helping narcissistic restoration of the couple as a "bad object" in order to make it into a "good object," but also to restore a natural ambivalent position with respect to it, whence comes the establishment of a climate of security, prompting an investment of trust in both the analyst and the analytic work.

But the silent partner listening to the speaker reacts and comments by means of non-verbal language (facial expressions, gesturing, even postures).

Analysts must be able to act between two attitudes: make possible, promote common verbalization of the poorly defined thoughts, affects underlying the conflicts and symptoms, as well as facilitating the expression and flow of fantasies by inviting each party to express what he or she sees as the conjugal psychic reality and that of his or her partner. And the latter will have to be able to hear it and react to it by conveying some impressions about what had been imagined, both about the couple and about his or her own psychic reality. But analysts will also have to protect the speaker's freedom to talk, by remaining silent.

The suffering couple 121

In addition, it is necessary for analysts to *make sure that individual boundaries are respected* and pay special attention to the possible danger connected with the damaging psychic penetration of one of the partners by the other.

Analysts also lend support to the chain of individual and conjugal associations when they detect that they are not in the service of the resistances to the group analytic process. They may help "reformulate" certain contents expressed, as well as encourage joint formulation of certain conflicts by the two partners, which will become a group formulation.

They thus adopt a "well-tempered," active position of essentially tactical value within a climate of security and narcissistic benevolence.

This fantasizing activity, as individual as it is conjugal, is in fact one of the expressions of this conjugal psychic reality, as well as corresponding to the interpretative activity of each of the partners. It will be able to involve each of the partners, their modes of communication, different events and situations of daily life in the home, as well as certain events of their life together or their respective families. However, underpinned by common anxiety, or for pathological or sociocultural reasons, the forms of expression of this representative activity within the couple can be inhibited. For example, since certain couples are not capable of this fantasizing, a veritable "lending of fantasies and words"[5] must take place, something which presupposes the analyst's ability to fantasize and give, something corresponding to Bion's (1962) "capacity for maternal reverie."[6]

The work of interpretation

This is a matter of interpreting each of the partners' transferential movements with respect to the analyst, as well as the predominant inter-transferential movements between the two partners, which structure their couple, and finally the transference of the conjugal group to the analyst.

But, first of all, I would like to indicate the wealth of open possibilities that compensate for the initial impression of being overwhelmed by the rush of stimuli and the complexity emanating from this "clinical living reality," something which presupposes the mobilization of capacities for analysis of the counter-transference on the part of analyst, as well as his or her creativity.

Let's consider again the three dimensions of the psychic conjugal reality: group, intersubjective and intrapsychic-individual.

Thus, the interpreting would focus on the *interplay of individual psychic processes in the group process as the expression of the functioning of the conjugal group* underlying it, in particular, the common and shared formations or conjugal formations of compromise, resistance, symptoms and blockages of psychic life. Thus, the obstacles standing in the way of thinking, feeling, imagining, engaging in exchanges about what one imagines, underpinned by anxieties aroused by some unconscious fantasies are an example of this type of resistance, as well as the blockages keeping the couple from carrying out its natural function of narcissistic support of each party, either directly or indirectly.

122 The suffering couple

Then, the interpretation concerns *detecting varied modalities of the intersubjective relationship* with its narcissistic, pregenital and œdipal overtones. The interplay of individual problems could take the form of unconscious distributions of roles such as those analyzed by Jürg Willi (1975)[7] and Jean Lemaire (1979).[8]

On the individual plane, unlike other colleagues, I consider that the reciprocal investment of the partner's psychic reality and functioning – one of the objects of my work – therefore, the discovery of certain finally verbalized aspects of his or her psychic life necessarily not involved in his or her conjugal life and, what is more, in this reassuring therapeutic, renarcissizing and relibidinalizing framework, can favor relational reorganizations through the suppression of ideas and fantasies having interpretative value and pathogenic repercussions, then proving mistaken.

The partners in fact constantly live with their interpretations – repressed, rationalized or denied, explicit or implicit, but always present and dangerously irrefutable – without any circumstances providing them with an opportunity to confront their own psychic reality and external reality, the partner's psychic reality. Finally, each one will be able to make his or her projections, interpretations and fantasies explicit and, as for the partner, he or she will be able to challenge them in order to reveal his or her own experience. Within this stimulating climate of flow of fantasies, the analyst will explain that these personal interpretations are imaginary productions providing information about the other person's psychic universe, whence comes their richness. Nevertheless, I shall keep an eye out for any possible perverse use by the latter.

Objectives and benefits

As concerns psychic reality, this work would usually make it possible to realize:

- A veritable "unsticking" of each of the partners by reducing excessive identification movements, in particular of an adhesive, projective and introjective kind, thus favoring a process of separation/individuation, then of subjectivization, in them, as well as a renarcissization expressing itself through greater autonomy.
- The acceptance of a certain degree of dependence upon the other and of invasion, both by the love-object and by the couple-object.
- A lowering of the level of conflictualities and less rigidity in their intersubjective relationship leading to making it more flexible, to its relibidinalization, to a better affective flow (reducing ambivalence and freeing tenderness, for example) and flow of fantasies, finally to a more open distribution of roles played alternatively by each one (father, mother, child, brother, sister, friend).
- An evolution of the representations of the love-object and of the couple-object, becoming then better integrated, and therefore less invasive.
- A redistribution of investments between the shared, common objects and the separate, individual objects. These changes will be able to motivate one or both partners to undertake individual work.

The effects of this psychic work will inevitably find expression in the bodily, sexual levels of reality, as well as in family (if it is also a matter of a parental couple) and social life.

The improvement or the resumption of sexual relations often accompanies this evolution, but is not steady. The investment of the bodies can evolve, finding expression in caring and concern for one another and seduction of one another.

The couple will discuss, notably, rearrangements (dynamic and economic) in the family, the repositioning of each person within the family group, the re-establishment of clear boundaries between the parental couple and the children, as well as talking about changes that have occurred in their "work couple" bringing about reorganizations of their home, professional reality, even of their various social relationships.

However, the evolution may be less patent, more limited, sectorial because of the existence of multiple, still irreducible, forms of resistance.

Finally, with or without success, certain couples decide to separate in the least heartrending manner possible.

My work with Martine and Louis

It has already been a year since Martine and Louis came to consult me regarding Louis' angry outbursts, which trouble considerably their life as a couple, becoming an object of conjugal conflict and revelatory of latent conflicts that we were going to discover together.

They have been together for ten years. However, they lived together for eight years and have been married for two years. Likeable, touching and intelligent, they demonstrate a very good level of verbalization and insight. In addition, they display tenderness and kindness in their exchanges. Contact with them is pleasant to me and I feel completely at ease.

At the end of our three preliminary, exploratory interviews, I propose psychoanalytic *couple work* to them and explain the framework. Indeed, my "overall" counter-transference finding expression in the impression of forming a "good therapeutic group with this couple" and by the feeling of being able to accomplish "good work" with them, therefore of helping them, determined my therapeutic decision.

Some biographical information

Martine, 35 years old, is an only child. Her parents separated when she was barely eight years old. However, she describes her father as always having been very absent, investing so little in his family life, his couple and his only child. With her mother she had what is called a symbiotic relationship and her maternal grandmother was particularly present in the home. After successful studies in a prestigious business school, she was very rapidly offered a job as directress of marketing in a well-regarded insurance company where she was still employed at the time. Her mother had a boyfriend, very invested by little Martine, who created his own business many years ago and had quite recently acquired prominent international standing. For her, he embodied an exemplary male father figure.

Louis, 40 years old, is the oldest of three children. He describes his parents as defective and conflictual from the time he was very young. His father, an engineer, very invested in his work, but fragile and submissive before his wife's sadism, had been drinking for far too long. After Louis was born, his mother had to interrupt her business studies, and therefore gave up her desire to become a senior executive. She grew depressed after the birth of her second child. Louis says that then he raised himself alone, invested a great deal in his school work and at home took care of his brother and sister, especially his sister who is ten years younger than he is. Nevertheless, he would tell us much later of displays of affection on the part of his father when he was very small, bringing him to say of him that "he was his God" at that time of his life. Louis is a computer engineer and presently works for a prestigious multinational firm.

Some indications of their choice of love-object

They seem to have essentially made a narcissistic object-choice, each one considering the other to be an idealized double of his- or herself: attractive, brilliant, admirable. Later on, I would discover other components of this choice, and therefore its greater complexity and richness:

- An œdipal component, Louis representing a mother figure, but also a powerful and reassuring father figure; Martine would represent a mother figure and undoubtedly an infantile figure of paternal admiration.
- A defensive component, protecting both from abandonment, castration, depressive and persecution anxieties.

Complaints, criticisms, objects of conflicts

Both work a great deal and fail to take much advantage of their free time. Martine in fact complains that Louis comes home late every evening, that they do not enjoy themselves and rarely go out together, and, above all, that he is reserved, not talking enough about how his day went, about his work, about his feelings, quite simply about himself. She finally decided to go out with her friends when he was not available. She tells how one evening, when Louis came home late, she ran out joyously to welcome him, but he told her he was exhausted and did not feel like talking. It made her feel rejected. "It's just that I couldn't, but I know that this hurts Martine." They make associations about their verbal exchanges, which she finds unsatisfactory. He also acknowledges that he likes Martine to wait for him, proof of his wife's love for him and cannot bear it when she is gone. "I know it's paradoxical." She then adds, "Now, I understand! Knowing that he needs half an hour to himself when he comes home, I decided to come home a half an hour later than he does!"

Louis explains that after a long day at work he needs a time of silence to take some necessary distance from both his excessively mentally demanding work and his wife. It is a time of mental restoration. Moreover, he thinks that work should not enter into his private space. There are different spaces and times to differentiate, to separate, without allowing contamination. He feels his wife's questions are intrusive and her requests invasive. This is why he must protect himself from these dangers by taking some distance, mainly achieved by his silence.

I would find that his wife's demands conjure up for him those of his mother, often issued as directives in an authoritarian manner. In this way, his wife would therefore represent a dangerous mother figure from whom he must protect himself. Martine does not understand Louis' need for silence, which she experiences and interprets as a form of rejection, a lack of interest in her, abandonment, reactivating the disinvestment and traumatic abandonment which her father inflicted upon her when she was a child, and which her mother, with whom "little Martine" identifies in this painful situation, also experienced. Moreover, with Louis, she re-enacts her need to establish an exclusive relationship with her mother.

Finally, I understand that Louis' angry outbursts express his inability to tell Martine, out of fear of hurting her, of his temporary need to remain a little alone in her presence by means of his protective, restorative silence, but also of the pressure of his fantasized expectations weighing on him. He is in fact afraid that she will interpret this as a kind of abandonment, indifference, and that she will then react aggressively. So, he restrains himself, holds back, then, after a while, when some insignificant situation arises, he explodes! My work to reformulate, to verbalize these affects, these fantasies and these interpretations enables me to clarify and correct their pathogenic mutual projections, enabling them to reduce considerably the frequency and intensity of these outbursts, making them pointless from then on. This opened the way to the verbalization of latent conflicts and things left unsaid, protected and kept at a distance by the manifest symptom of "Louis' angry outbursts." Before looking at them, let us note that within the context of sibling rivalry, "being the better of the two," expression of the reactivation of their sibling complexes, Louis' angry outbursts are to Martine's advantage in that they reassure her of her worth in a transferential movement directed toward me, representing then a parental figure. She was saying to herself: "There, at least, he is falling short. I am the better of the two." She was therefore benefitting narcissistically, just as he was deriving satisfaction of a sadomasochistic nature, attacking a mother figure; however, by the same token, degenerating narcissistically and masochistically in relationship to the woman who also admires him. Consequently, sadomasochistic interplay is also at work, indicating the existence of a pregenital level of their intersubjective relationship. The three levels of their conjugal relationship, narcissistic, pregenital and œdipal are thus revealed.

The conflict about the desire for a child

Let us now come back to another latent object of conflict that came to light in the course of my work, that of the desire for a child, which takes on different meanings for each of them, bearer(s) of hard to verbalize anxieties.

126 The suffering couple

Thus, for Louis, it would, on the one hand, be a matter of being a good father, better than his own father, with the desire to outperform him, then, from this œdipal perspective, to present a child to his mother, to take the place of the defective father and correlatively to assert himself as a better husband. On the other hand, he is animated by a desire to repair a father figure who is loved, admired and wounded all at the same time. Finally, the child that he fantasizes would represent Martine identified with a little girl: therefore his narcissistic, infantile double.

For Martine, this child would be a rival, because she also sees herself as Louis' one and only child, mother figure, but also father figure, reparative of early traumatic wounds. She would then have to share this twofold love with the child who therefore represents a danger because it would rob her of her status as an only child within their couple. She has in fact always been a little girl in her own eyes and must remain pampered by her husband and by her mother (future grandmother) who might then abandon her daughter. Martine therefore perceives a risk of losing narcissistic benefits. "I don't feel ready." This is also to be understood as, "I don't feel ready to be a mother like my mother," and therefore to take her place and have a child by him, something which represents a danger of an œdipal nature.

Once we resumed our sessions following a vacation, Martine came back to this saying that she had given it thought. She believed she had always protected herself from men and from the danger of their leaving, but at the same time, she had set up conditions permitting her to leave if problems arose. That is why the fact of having a child would tie her to a man and keep her from being free and autonomous. She makes an association with disillusionment recently inflicted upon her by her father, then with his leaving home when she was eight years old. She is afraid of being abandoned by the man to whom she could become attached. But she has been able to trust Louis who represents both a reliable mother figure, always present and there for her, but also an ideal, non-abandoning father figure. He will not abandon her as her father did, even if they do not have a child. So here she has therefore verbalized her fear of reliving the disinvestment and traumatic abandon experienced in her childhood, as well as the function of repairing these early wounds that she has not worked through, something which must be accomplished by and in her couple. Nevertheless, let us also note that in being able to leave, Martine is identifying with her father.

The anal object-relation particularly pronounced in Louis is also expressed in his suffering tied to his incapacity to have any kind of "hold" on Martine's love. He feels frustrated, even narcissistically wounded. He can then verbalize his need to be the center of Martine's attention and interest, thus identifying himself with his father's desire in relationship to his wife, but probably also with the only child that he was for a while with his mother, in particular. Unfortunately, his father failed with his wife who was quite frustrating. She grew depressed, while he turned to alcohol and hyperinvested in his work, seeking in it satisfactions, narcissistic ones especially, lacking at home. Consequently, one finds that Louis, demanding love and mastery, is re-enacting this parental situation with Martine who would try to thwart this, given the history of her relations with her father. In this, she would be embodying a frustrating and unsatisfactory mother figure.

Finally, Louis also experienced early narcissistic wounds that he has not worked out, awaiting treatment and reparation through the couple he forms with Martine. Consequently, both find themselves facing common problems of abandonment, early wounds, symbiotico-fusional needs and a need for exclusive love. I finally learn that the desire for a child, the family project that "cements" the couple, to use Louis' expression, was taboo. He has desired this for a long time and she does not feel ready. "With respect to that, I feel frustrated," he says. He is placed in a woman's position in relation to Martine who, in this situation, would be playing a man's role, postponing plans for a child, frustrating because she has represented to herself an aspect of her father. So, we could imagine that Louis' angry outbursts derive from this frustration, non-verbalized up until then, enabling him to express his hostility and making her pay for the pain of his frustration.

Some components in the organization of their conjugal life

Focusing on his work and his conjugal life with Martine, above all at home, Louis seems to have organized his life along obsessional and masochistic lines. Not much leisure and vacation time. He is the one who directs their home life, distributes the roles and tasks to be performed, especially attending to housework and tidying up, but also to administrative affairs, while Martine is particularly responsible for ironing and shopping, displaying "stinginess," like Louis' mother, it seems. Moreover, it is she who organizes outings and trips. He is the "home secretary" (domestic dictator) and she the "secretary of external affairs" (oriented toward people, friends, outings, trips)! They have few common leisure activities because he is very tired and needs to sleep during the weekend, partially devoted to shopping and housework. Louis has few friends because he does not really feel the need. Martine in fact concentrates his investments as a whole alongside those mobilized by his work. She would represent his wife as well as his best friend. That is why, it is, above all, Martine's friends whom they socialise with together or she alone, separately, when he is not available. In this way, they keep one another from benefitting from their very good income and their success. Is some common, shared unconscious guilt playing a determinant role and underlying the "punitive" and masochistic organization of their conjugal life?

She reproaches him for only wanting to talk about intellectual, intelligent subjects and would also like them to be like two girlfriends, talking about anything at all, going shopping together, for example, mobilizing her female homosexual component that would call upon Louis' femininity, something that he does not consciously desire.

Moreover, she dreams that he will one day create and direct a prestigious company. And this conscious fantasy of professional success, of excellence, is common and shared, but seems to enter into conflict with a probable unconscious fantasy of castration, expression of their common œdipal guilt.

In the course of the work, they have both formulated a request for individual work while pursuing our work together.

128 The suffering couple

Transfero-counter-transferential movements

The basic transference, of good quality, is expressed by basic confidence in me, their therapist. The multiple transferential movements are, above all, intersubjective and also involve the conjugal group. I represent a good, containing mother and a kindly Superego father, protective and structuring. On the counter-transferential level, I feel a certain harmony with what has been aroused by each one and by the conjugal group.

Martine appears to be a young, charming, firm, mischievous, funny woman. Louis is a young, well-educated man, intelligent, touching, animated by a desire for mastery. The couple seems to me likeable, vibrant, motivated, invested in this work, suggestive of two children in difficulty. They display good insight, a critical attitude and mutual kindliness. I feel at ease, capable of identifying with both Martine and Louis, thus mobilizing my psychic bisexuality, but also lending each one narcissistic support when I deem it necessary. Our relationship is flexible, nuanced and interspersed with humor. My group counter-transference finds expression in the feeling of being a good therapist whose thinking is sharpened, lively and creative, which tells me about their conjugal psychic reality animated by a fantasy of omnipotence and excellence. We do indeed form a "good therapeutic group."

Some elements of understanding

Exploring the three levels of their conjugal psychic reality

In the first place, let us discuss the group level. Their common and shared psychic reality is organized, especially, by fantasies, parental imagos and unconscious structuring, defensive, but also offensive, alliances.

A fantasy of omnipotence – stimulating a common ideal of success and professional excellence giving way to creation of an offensive alliance – coexists and enters into conflict with a fantasy of castration, expression of common œdipal guilt, finding expression in a punitive masochistic organization of their conjugal life. I have also detected a defensive fantasy of a symbiotico-fusional couple, protecting itself from anxieties of abandonment correlative to early narcissistic wounds that have not been worked out and are waiting to be treated and repaired within the couple by what are called defensive (denegative pact) alliances.

What about the parental imagos? In Martine, the maternal imago is powerful and omnipresent; the paternal imago is weak, but the man must be powerful, because there is a danger of temptation of castration. In Louis, the paternal imago is weak, masochistic and the maternal imago is depressive, but also sadistic and castrating.

Among the common psychic formations, I have identified a "conjugal Self," a narcissistic structure, particularly "hyperthrophied," a "conjugal Ego" stimulated and fed by the narcissistic structure, but crushed by a rather tyrannical "Ideal of the conjugal Ego" and establishing a sadomasochistic relationship with the limitative "conjugal Superego."

They construct different representations of their couple-object or "couple fantasy" and of their relationship to this object.

"A couple is a place where one can say everything to one another, exchange and share the good things and the bad things. It is also a place where one can find fulfillment. If not, it is of no interest to me," declares Martine. While for Louis, it is a fortress, a place of protection. He does not, therefore, want to talk about professional problems in order to protect Martine and their couple from disruptive elements. But, it is also an invasive object from which one must protect oneself, by setting time limits and by silence, especially. I therefore understand Martine, who suffers from not sufficiently sharing their daily lives with Louis and feels lonely in this regard. Nonetheless, they come together through the sharing of a common representation, that of a space and an omnipotent narcissistic object reparative of early wounds that are still alive.

What can be said of their intersubjective relationship? It involves distinct elements of object-relation of the oral and anal kind, phallic and genital aspects being quite obviously present. Narcissistic aspects are also very pronounced, as I have indicated, both of them especially finding themselves constrained to sustain mutual admiration. Both the projective and the introjective identification movements are massive. As I have already mentioned, each one's Œdipus and sibling complexes have been revived and related to one another within their conjugal relationship. Let us note the pronounced sibling component, each one being able to represent a bisexual, narcissistic double for the other one

Individually speaking, they differ with regard to their relationship and their mode of investment as a couple. Louis seems to protect himself more from this than Martine, but, paradoxically, limits his principal investments to his wife, his couple and his work, unlike Martine, who diversifies them more broadly.

The couple's bisexuality

Martine is re-enacting her pre-œdipal relationship and her negative Œdipus complex with Louis, put in a maternal position, and in her service exclusively. She has lived in a world of women where men are absent and denigrated, except for her mother's boyfriend, creator and head of a company. With Louis, she identifies with her mother's little girl, but also with the man of the house who is served by his wife, who does not always desire to have a child and is disorderly, causing himself to be reprimanded by his wife. She would like to have him play the role of girlfriend, go window-shopping and talk about clothes or about anything whatsoever, which he refuses to do. Louis also considers Martine to be "his best buddy." Moreover, he accepts the role of mother, identifying himself and repairing his own defective mother imago, but by identifying with Martine, he also receives fantasized satisfactions connected with care provided by a good mother. By identifying with the defective

130 The suffering couple

paternal imago, he also frustrates Martine. He is thus capable of satisfying and frustrating his wife.

A failure of couple work

How are we to understand the signs of suffering in this couple in terms of the failure of *couple work*? Certain aspects of their conjugal psychic functioning – especially the constraining fantasy of omnipotence accompanied by a constant desire for mutual admiration in a conflictual relationship with a castration fantasy, as well as anxieties connected with the symbiotico-fusional couple fantasy and the correlative defensive measures, the latent things left unsaid and conflicts – had harmful effects of isolation, inhibition and impoverishment on their intersubjective relationship and upon each other, something which had a determinant effect on their "work couple" in the home, for example, as well as on their social and professional life: multiple pressures, invasive restrictions and failings, leading them to a masochistic, "punitive" organization of their conjugal life. I know nothing, moreover, about their sexual life.

Some changes made through our work

Bringing to light certain fantasies organizing their common psychic reality, diverse unconscious alliances, certain conflicts and things left unsaid, combined with an effort to work them out, in particular enabled them to:

- make their "conjugal Ego Ideal" and "conjugal Superego" more flexible;
- especially, reduce the number of constraints and inhibitions prevailing in their intersubjective relationship, to make it more comfortable and tranquil, which has found expression in richer and more diversified verbal communication.

In addition, their relationship to their couple-object has also evolved.

Moreover, changes have been introduced into their social and professional life. Martine and Louis give one another more time together, meet more often with friends and seem to invest in their work a bit less.

While Martine engaged in individual work, Louis seems to have personally benefited from working as a couple, also using it as a kind of individual therapy in the presence of his spouse. I had already observed this manner of using couple therapy by one of the partners, which indirectly shows the existence of a symbiotic mode of conjugal functioning.

Martine and Louis' couple therapy thus confers upon them the means to engage in *couple work* that will enable them to make change in the three realities – psychic, sexual-bodily and socio-cultural – that they will experience from then on in a much more satisfactory way than before.

Notes

1 Jean-Georges Lemaire (1998), *Les mots du couple*. Paris: Payot.
2 *Ibid.*
3 *Op. cit.*, Grunberger.
4 *Op. cit.*, Anzieu.
5 *Op. cit.*, Lemaire, *Les mots du couple.*
6 *Op. cit.*, Bion, *Learning from Experience.*
7 *Op. cit.*, Willi, *Couples in Collusion.*
8 *Op. cit.*, Lemaire, *Le couple, sa vie, sa mort.*

By way of conclusion

At the close of this attempt to undertake a pluri- and interdisciplinary investigation of couples, have I succeeded in sketching a unified and intelligible general, though inevitably heterogeneous, account? First of all, I wished to disclose, to bring to light, all the complexity of this composite, sexual-bodily, psychic and socio-cultural living reality, with diverse and variable interrelationships. It evolves in accordance with a complex temporality resulting from the intertwining of tempo-ralities proper to each of these realities, which is an additional factor contributing to its complexity and conflictuality.

This conjugal reality is "dynamic," "economic," "topographical" and historical. Indeed, while it is traversed by a plurality of currents of antagonistic instinctual investments that have already been taken into consideration, it is also animated by multiple conflictualities, both internal and external, which I have particularly explored and which are in an ongoing state of tension with one another.

The inner conflictualities are structural, psychic (intra- and inter-) in nature, integrating the interiorization of cultural factors, and only psychoanalysis can pro-vide us access to them because they are unconscious.

Being intrinsic to all structuring and all functioning of couples, they can be attenuated, obliterated, repressed, even denied, split and projected upon certain elements of the couple's external reality, as well as expressed, amplified, even exacerbated, depending on the historical, social and cultural characteristics of any society to which the couple belongs, and especially in times of crisis and social change. I shall come back to this.

The construction, then the durability, of a couple presupposes, in fact, negotia-tion, attenuation, repression, even the denial of its diverse primordial conflictualities between: Ego/love-object, Ego/couple-object, identity/alterity, narcissism/objec-tality, Eros/destructive drive, self-preservation/sexuality, pregenitality/genitality, male/female, psychic bisexuality/sexual identity, couple/external reality, private couple/public couple, especially. Intrapsychic and intersubjective compromises will therefore necessarily have to be at work, themselves dynamic and economic in nature, meaning shifting, and variable, and therefore fragile. This is why a psycho-analytical understanding of "conjugal conflicts" must first imperatively conceive every couple as a living reality, immersed in a world external to it, source of

By way of conclusion 133

beneficial and harmful phenomena. Insufficient compromises, the prevalence of individual and/or conjugal "quantitative," economic factors due to the lack of mastery of critical situations, for example, can determine individual and/or conjugal psychic suffering that will find expression in the emergence of so-called "conjugal conflicts" situated on one or several levels of conjugal reality: psychic, sexual-bodily and socio-cultural. They will assume forms using the diversified modes of communication, whether variable or ritualized, but will also be able to be latent, unconscious obstacles hindering their exteriorization. While they "noisily" attest to every couple's essential conflictual dynamic, they may also represent, because of their ongoing nature, more or less marked failures of *couple work*. These conflictualities erupt when there is a crisis and provoke crises while they are erupting.

For their part, external conflictualities, tense among themselves, are historically and socio-culturally variable, certain of them being predominant during one era or another.

J-C. Bologne (2005),[1] historian, brought out well these major conflicts of interest among the external powers represented by families, the states and the churches that have entered into conflict with the repressed aspirations of the individuals concerned and attempted to control the conjugal institution. Nonetheless, he also identified their role as guarantors of durability, of protection ensuring a certain stability to this marital union, whether it be social, political, financial, familial or psychological. This is no longer the case, or very insufficiently so, in our contemporary society. Would they have had this power to control and contain, even stifle the conflictualities intrinsic to every couple? This is probable, but how was this possible? As I have recounted, traditional marriage was long based on a social bond and not on a free individual choice of the partner determined by feelings of love, something which can attenuate certain types of structural antagonisms and foster projective reactions onto external objects of conflicts: "Our problems are caused by our families," for example.

It seems to me that our Western society's evolution toward the prevalence of individualism has been necessarily accompanied by a distinct weakening of those historically traditional powers (families, the states, the churches) in contrast to other contemporary societies.

However, what does present-day research by historians, demographers, sociologists, anthropologists and psychoanalysts have to teach us?

These specialists emphasize the historical and mutative transition from an institutional, traditional definition of the couple, through marriage, to an internal, largely intersubjective definition of the contemporary couple that is no longer guaranteed, or so little so, by the institutions.

In addition, contemporary couples have become unstable, fragile, polymorphous and demanding. They have a harder and harder time lasting, despite their combined narcissistic desire to be eternal and exclusive that underpins their initial "conjugal contract," something to which a number of studies and statistics have attested since the 1970s: the drop in the rate of heterosexual nuptiality, the increased numbers of hetero- and homosexual people living together, divorces and

134 By way of conclusion

separations, homosexual marriages, civil unions, "polyamorous arrangements" and, above all, the reduction in the number of couples said to be "cohabiting" and the increased number of persons living alone, especially in the big international metropolises. However, for all that, these people are neither without sexuality, nor without partners. They have chosen a less committed, and therefore looser, conjugal arrangement characteristic of contemporary couples.

Moreover, the numerous requirements each person has for the love-object and the couple have become multifold: sexual; communicational ("we have to talk about everything," "we must not hide anything from one another"); intellectual; relating to identity (reinforcement of intimate, statutory-professional and sexual components); psychic (love in the form of tenderness, narcissistic support, concern for the other person, support in difficult times, but also spaces–times of restorative regression, for repairing early psychic wounds, for each person's self-fulfillment). Consequently, the couple must above all not be an occasion for frustrations and suffering. Moreover, this excess of mutual requirements and expectations for the couple and the loving partner combine with the joint force of relations between the sexes that have become egalitarian and demanding in regard to both individuality and identity. From this comes the existence of a conflict of ideal requirements and representations between those linked to the individual (man and woman) and those linked to the couple. All this grows more complex with the creation of a family, because other types of conflict occur: couple/family, loving couple/parental couple, individual/family.

Our contemporary couples are typical representatives of our Western society, which has become distinctly individualistic and permeated with paradoxical "trends." Consequently, they are "symptomatic" of a society that is clearly suffering and, moreover, pathogenic, which is what I find in my practice as a psychoanalyst and therapist for couples.

How do anthropologists and sociologists characterize this? Among their observations, we should mention, in particular:

- *The new centrality of sexuality*, henceforth inscribed at the heart of the sphere of conjugal intimacy and affectivity. This becomes a basic personal practice in the construction of the subject, masculine as well as feminine, as well as a conjugal practice building and consolidating the couple. Its shortcomings today represent a factor threatening rupture. And, on that level, I find a convergence of expectations and demands of men and women, notably for "sexual continuity," historically new, principally before the birth of children. Besides, sexuality is, nowadays, the object of multifold dissociation:
  - o Procreation henceforth occupies a specific, limited position place.
  - o Sexuality tends also to be disconnected from marriage or from conjugality, from feelings of love and from the emotional dimension, more generally.
  - o A separation is also taking place between erotic sexuality, with the fantasized, "retentive" dimension of desire[2] and the sexuality-release, discharging

excitation, suggestive of an expulsive anal component with fecalization of the object of the desire.

- ○ Finally, considering the social pressure and, especially, that of the mass media, a new separation is taking place between erotic sexuality and hygienic sexuality. "Sex is good for health, like participating in sports!" One must therefore practise sex!

  However, our specialists and observers of social reality agree in thinking that a conjugal relationship based exclusively, or principally focused on the sexual dimension, is doomed, because sex is unstable by definition. Indeed, the couple proves to be a "high-risk zone" when it comes to sexual desire, the managing of which remains one of the major problems of couples who last and age as time goes by.

- *Our society's particularly marked movement toward medicalization and psychologization*, whose discourse and practices produce beliefs, new normative models of thinking and conduct, often interpreted, then conveyed by the different mass media.
- *The values of mobility, of change* that discredit the ideas of permanence and long-term planning. Yet, this contemporary value of mobility conflicts with that of being lasting.
- *The decline of institutions and hierarchies, the relative disappearance of outward morality and of its norms of conduct*, progressively replaced by "principles of inner regulation" leading to a morality that has become strictly private.

In the end, our society would convey to us prescriptions that are paradoxical, pathogenic in nature, that we, as well as couples and families, shall all have to come to terms with, such as:

- Be an adult and responsible, mature/remain young and preserve the "freshness" of childhood.
- Be a man, make the most of your virility/but also be able to express your femininity; be a woman, develop your femininity/but, express masculine, phallic traits accorded value nowadays.
- Be accomplished, fulfill yourself personally, think of yourself/live reciprocity, sharing, altruism.
- Be spontaneous/display self-control and self-mastery.
- Be mobile, change, evolve/be stable, invest in the long-term.
- Take advantage of immediate pleasures, live in the present, do not worry about anything/make plans, prepare for the future.

The psychoanalyst's first reflections

All that suggests to the psychoanalyst a predominance of narcissistic and pregenital elements, of primary psychic processes, of an omnipotent pleasure principle

136 By way of conclusion

combining with a dwindling of œdipal factors, of secondary psychic processes, of sublimation and symbolization, that in this way are evidence of a society characterized by distinctly narcissistic and perverse elements. This is the reason for which the present-day evolution of couples toward breaking up early, the multiplicity of conjugal unions within the life of one subject, loose and looser forms of organization, celibacy, which does not, moreover, serve as a role model, but also the absence, or the requirement, of desire for a child, sometimes late, seem to me to be typical symptoms of our society with its pathogenic paradoxical "trends" and traits.

The already mentioned structural conflictualities of every couple would then be exacerbated, for some of them, by certain of these fundamental characteristics of our society. Indeed, the increasingly dual situation of couples, henceforth alone responsible for their future, has made them lose their historical institutional framework, often so oppressive, that symbolic third party, also protector and agent of a structuring œdipal triangulation, guaranteeing them stability and durability. Of course, but to the detriment of their identity existence, due to their alienation from families, states and religious institutions. It would be desirable to look for a satisfactory middle course. And, what if these characteristics of our society and of our couples were also those of one of the numerous, inevitable critical periods of Western history, therefore bringing, in the early stages, changes?

Complementary reflections

Our society is "in crisis" and, because of that, is undergoing evolution, with rapid and quasi-ongoing changes, owing to its auto- and reorganizing systemic aspects that have become "hypercomplex" according to the sociologist Edgar Morin (1984).[3] It is experiencing rupture, correlative of a failure of "work of continuity" performed by the cultural heritage, and disorganizing–reorganizing transformations that are fragilizing, attacking and shaking its principal "metapsychic" and "metasocial" guarantors (families, the churches, the states, models of thought and of conduct, especially), and our contemporary couples are quite obviously caught in this uncontrollable historical, socio-cultural turbulence, swept up in these disintegrating–reintegrating trends, social forces of disjoining and rejoining. Consequently, have our fragile, unstable, shifting and polymorphous contemporary couples also become "hypercomplex," integrating, therefore, the properties of "hypercomplexity"? What is the impact of this on *couple work* and its new forms? Is the notion of failure pertinent then? Does it remain so? And if the answer is yes, according to which criteria?

Allow me to recall briefly that *couple work* is an interdisciplinary concept endeavoring to account for, in a consistent, unified manner, the different levels of reality that every couple experiences, requiring that its members, therefore, work within each one of these common, shared realities (psychic, sexual-bodily and socio-cultural), as well as within their interrelationships, but also in coordination with that realized by the conjugal partner. However, this *couple work* realized conjointly by the Ego of each partner is inevitably found in an antagonistic dynamic

By way of conclusion 137

relationship with the "individual work" serving the subject. One of any couple's fundamental conflicts between the "individual interests" and the "interests of the couple" reappears in this way. What share will each party devote, or rather will he or she desire and be able to devote to the couple, without experiencing personal danger? A question all the more paradoxical since, on the one hand, our society places value on individuals and their interests within the unprecedented framework of equality of the sexes, but nevertheless elevates the couple to a central point of reference (to be differentiated from the conjugal intersubjective relation), while celibacy would not represent a model way of life, and, on the other hand, conjugal durability is conditioned by the very quality of this joint *couple work*. This problem of lasting is all the more important since feelings of boredom threaten every couple and, with the increasing life span, conjugal aging is one of the things on the horizon. So, I think, all the same, that suffering, dissatisfaction, early conjugal rupture and increasing multiplication of new couples are patent signs of a failure of *couple work*, especially through joint, even unilateral, insufficiency and are made all the more difficult through the fragility, even the breakdown, of its traditional symbolic guarantors and the absence of substitute points of reference.

Among the factors of durability associated with the psychic dimension of *couple work*, allow me to mention:

- The paracritical, containing, structuring envelope constituted by the couple's "metapsychic" and "metasocial" guarantors.[4]
- The maintaining of an ambivalent, narcissistic investment of the love-object and the couple-object.
- The current of tenderness and ongoing mutual narcissistic reinforcement.
- The utilization of a sublimated homosexual investment in the "conjugal friendship."
- The mobilization of individual and conjugal creativity.
- But also the participation of "good masochism," "guardian of conjugal life," meaning of the pooling of the couple's primary erogenous masochistic nucleus, enabling the construction of a "satisfactory conjugal masochistic arrangement" that plays a determinant role in the expectation, tolerance of frustrations, in the deferment of "conjugal" satisfaction, and in managing critical movements, in particular. However, I am observing the opposite situation more and more frequently in today's couples. In witnessing the urgency and immediacy of forms of pleasure, the difficulty in deferring them, the difficulty in the capacity to wait, as well as the different place occupied by the said "conjugal conflicts," which are perceived nowadays as threatening and being able to trigger a breakup. Furthermore, I observe a crisis in identity models, through the attack upon their metapsychic and metasocial guarantors. The traditional model of their parental couples, one of their necessary and inevitable sources of inspiration, conflicts and competes with their desire to free themselves from it in order to invent, create their "conjugal model" responding strictly to individual and subjectivizing aspirations, as well as in "conformity" with the new

By way of conclusion

models conveyed by the mass media. From this comes a contemporary crisis of "conjugal models" that is producing changes and transformations finding expression in the emergence of multiple forms of conjugalities.

Finally, correlatively, for several years, I have observed a growing number of couples coming to consult me for diverse types of suffering. These consultations, early or not, attest not only to a failure of *couple work* but also to more pronounced contemporary concern accorded to the quality of conjugal life, as well as expectations and requirements with regard to it unprecedented up until now in Western history.

At this point in my exploratory journey, I remain ever more conscious of the complexity of this composite living reality – exposed and subject to socio-cultural, psychic and historical turbulences – and of the difficulties standing in the way of any comprehensive, intelligible grasp of it. Nevertheless, my attempt to engage in this pluri- and interdisciplinary investigation, "an initial setting in order and giving shape to," has enabled me to advance noticeably and to catch sight of some happy prospects. Work will necessarily have to be undertaken in two directions: that of an investigation into the epistemology of interdisciplinarity in the social sciences and humanities and that of fruitful pluri- and interdisciplinary collaboration.

Notes

1 *Op. cit.*, Bologne.
2 *Op. cit.*, Fain and Braunschweig.
3 Edgar Morin (1984), *Sociologie*. Paris: Fayard, 1994.
4 *Op. cit.*, Kaës, *Les alliances inconscientes*.

Bibliography

André, J. (1995). *Aux origines féminines de la sexualité*. Paris: Presses universitaires de France, 2004.

Anzieu, D. (1975). *The Group and the Unconscious*. London: Routledge, 1999. Originally published as *Le groupe et l'inconscient*. Paris: Dunod.

Balint, M. (1956). *Primary Love and Psycho-analytic Technique*. London: Karnac, 1985.

Balint, M. (1967). *The Basic Fault*. London: Routledge, 2013

Benveniste, E. (1973). *Indo-European Language and Society*. Coral Gables, FL: University of Miami Press.

Bion, W.R. (1961). *Experiences in Groups and Other Papers*. London: Tavistock. Reprint of W. R. Bion (1952), "Group dynamics: A review," *International Journal of Psycho-Analysis*, vol. 33.

Bion, W.R. (1962). *Learning from Experience*. New York: Basic Books.

Bollas, C. (1989). *Forces of Destiny: Psychoanalysis and the Human Idiom*. London: Free Association Books.

Bologne, J-C. (2005). *Histoire du mariage en Occident*. Paris: Hachette.

Bouvet, M. (1960). *La relation d'objet*. Paris: Presses universitaires de France, 2006.

Bozon, M. (2009). *Sociologie de la sexualité*. Paris: Armand Colin.

Burguière, A. (1986). "La formation du couple," in A. Burguière, C. Klapisch-Zuber, M. Ségalen and F. Zonabend (eds), *Histoire de la famille*, vol. 3, *Le choc des modernités*. Paris: Armand Colin, pp. 147–88. English translation: *History of the Family*. Cambridge, MA: Bellknap, 1996.

Brusset, B. (2007). *Psychanalyse du lien*. Paris: Presses universitaires de France.

Bydlowski, M. (2008). *Les enfants du désir*. Paris: Odile Jacob.

Caillot, J-P. and Decherf, G. (1989). *Psychanalyse du couple et de la famille*. Paris: A. PSY.G.-Editions.

Cournut, J. (2001). *Pourquoi les hommes ont peur des femmes*. Paris: Presses universitaires de France, 2006.

Danon-Boileau, H. (2000). *De la vieillesse à la mort*. Paris: Hachette.

David, C. (1992). *La bisexualité psychique*. Paris: Payot & Rivages, 1997.

de Singly, F. (2004). *Le soi, le couple et la famille*. Paris: Nathan.

Dicks, H. V. (1967). *Marital Tensions. Clinical Studies towards a Psychological Theory of Interaction*. New York: Basic Books.

Durkheim, E. (1893). *Division of Labor in Society*. New York: Free Press, 1997.

Eiguer, A. (1998). *Clinique psychanalytique du couple*. Paris: Dunod.

140 Bibliography

Elias, N. (1939). *Über den Prozess der Zivilization*. Basel: Haus zum Falken. English translation: *The Civilizing Process: Sociogenetic and Psychogenetic Investigations*. Oxford: Blackwell Publishers, 2000 (revised edition).

Fain, M. and Braunschweig, D. (1971). *Eros et Antéros, Réflexions psychanalytiques sur la sexualité*. Paris: Payot.

Fairbairn, W. R. D. (1995). *From Instinct to Self: Selected Papers* (vol 1: Clinical and Theoretical Papers). Lanham (Maryland): Jason Aronson, Inc.

Faure-Pragier, S. (1998). *Les bébés de l'inconscient, Le psychanalyste face aux stérilités féminines aujourd'hui*. Paris: Presses universitaires de France.

Ferenczi, S. (1931). "Confusion of tongues between adults and the child" (1933), in *Final Contributions to the Problems and Methods of Psychoanalysis*. London: Hogarth Press, 1955, pp. 156–67.

Freud, S. (1905). *Three Essays on the Theory of Sexuality*. *S.E.*, 7. London: Hogarth.

Freud, S. (1912). *On the Universal Tendency to Debasement in the Sphere of Love*. *S.E.*, 11. London: Hogarth.

Freud, S. (1914a). *On Narcissism: An Introduction*. *S.E.*, 14. London: Hogarth.

Freud, S. (1914b). *Remembering, Repeating and Working-through*. *S.E.*, 12. London: Hogarth.

Freud, S. (1915a). *Observations on Transference-Love*. *S.E.*, 12. London: Hogarth.

Freud, S. (1915b). *Thoughts for the Times on War and Death*. *S.E.*, 14. London: Hogarth.

Freud, S. (1915c). *Instincts and Their Vicissitudes*. *S.E.*, 14. London: Hogarth.

Freud, S. (1916–17). *Introductory Lectures on Psycho-Analysis* (Part III). *S.E.*, 16. London: Hogarth.

Freud, S. (1917). *Mourning and Melancholia*. *S.E.*, 14, London: Hogarth.

Freud, S. (1918). *The Taboo of Virginity*. *S.E.*, 11. London: Hogarth.

Freud, S. (1920). *The Psychogenesis of a Case of Female Homosexuality*. *S.E.*, 18. London: Hogarth.

Freud, S. (1921). *Group Psychology and the Analysis of the Ego*. *S.E.*, 18. London: Hogarth.

Freud, S. (1922). *Some Neurotic Mechanisms in Jealousy, Paranoia and Homosexuality*. *S.E.*, 18. London: Hogarth.

Freud, S. (1923). *The Ego and the Id*. *S.E.*, 19. London: Hogarth.

Freud, S. (1924a). *The Economic Problem of Masochism*. *S.E.*, 19, London: Hogarth.

Freud, S. (1924b). *The Dissolution of the Oedipus Complex*. *S.E.*, 19, London: Hogarth.

Freud, S. (1925). *Some Psychical Consequences of the Anatomical Distinction between the Sexes*. *S.E.*, 19. London: Hogarth.

Freud, S. (1927). *Fetishism*. *S.E.*, 21. London: Hogarth.

Freud, S. (1930). *Civilization and Its Discontents*. *S.E.*, 21. London: Hogarth.

Freud, S. (1931). *Female Sexuality*. *S.E.*, 21. London: Hogarth.

Freud, S. (1933). *Femininity. Lecture XXXIII of New Introductory Lectures*. *S.E.*, 22, London: Hogarth.

Garcia, V. (2007). "Le couple: un lieu pour se réparer?" in Serge Arpin (ed.), *Le divan familial, Rencontres entre Familles et Culture*. Paris: Les Editions In Press, pp. 89–102.

Godelier, M. (2004). *Métamorphoses of Kinship*. London: Verso, 2011. Translation of *Métamorphoses de la parenté*. Paris: Fayard, 2004.

Green, A. (1983). *Life Narcissism, Death Narcissism*. London: Free Association Books, 2001. Translation of *Narcissisme de vie, narcissisme de mort*. Paris: Les Editions de Minuit, 1983.

Green, A. (1997). *The Chains of Eros, The Sexual in Psychoanalysis*. London: Karnac, 2008. Translation of *Les chaînes d'Eros, l'actualité du sexuel*, Paris, Odile Jacob, 1997.

Bibliography 141

Grunberger, B. (1971). *Le narcissisme*. Paris: Payot & Rivages, 1993. English translation: *Narcissism: Psychoanalytic Essays*. Madison, CT: International Universities Press, 1979.

Héritier, F. (1996). *Masculin/Féminin. La pensée de la différence*. Paris: Odile Jacob.

Kaës, R. (1989). "Le Pacte dénégatif. Eléments pour une métapsychologie des ensembles transsubjectifs," in A. Missenard and G. Rosolato (eds), *Figures et modalités du négatif*. Paris: Dunod. pp. 101–36.

Kaës, R. (2007). *Un singulier pluriel*. Paris: Dunod.

Kaës, R. (2008). *Le complexe fraternel*. Paris: Dunod.

Kaës, R. (2009). *Les alliances inconscientes*. Paris: Dunod.

Kaufmann, J-C. (2007). *Sociologie du couple*. Paris: Presses universitaires de France.

Klein, M. (1937). "Love, guilt and reparation," in Melanie Klein and Joan Riviere, *Love, Hate and Reparation*. New York: W. W. Norton, 1964, pp. 57–119.

Klein, M. (1957). "Envy and gratitude," in *Envy and Gratitude and Other Works*. London: Random House, 1997, pp. 176–236.

Lebovici, S. (2002). "Entretien de L. Solis-Ponton avec Serge Lebovici," in L. Solis-Ponton (ed.), *La parentalité*. Paris: Presses universitaires de France, pp. 7–21.

Le Gouès, G. (2000). *L'âge et le principe de plaisir: introduction à la clinique tardive*. Paris: Dunod.

Lemaire, J-G. (1979). *Le couple, sa vie, sa mort*. Paris: Payot.

Lemaire, J-G. (1998). *Les mots du couple*. Paris: Payot.

Littré, E. (2007). *Dictionnaire de la langue française*. Paris: Encyclopedia Universalis.

Luquet, P. (2003). *Les identifications*. Paris: Presses universitaires de France.

Masters, W. H. and Johnson, V. (1966). *Human Sexual Response*. Toronto: Bantam Books, 1981.

Mauss, M. (1924). "Essai sur le don," in *Sociologie et anthropologie*. Paris: Presses universitaires de France, 1950, pp. 145–279.

Morin, E. (1984). *Sociologie*. Paris: Fayard, 1994.

Parat, C. (1967). "L'organisation œdipienne du stade génital, Rapport au congrès des psychanalystes de langues françaises," *Revue française de psychanalyse*, vol. 31, no. 5–6 (September–December).

Pichon-Rivière, E. (1965). *El proceso grupal. Del psicoanalisis a la psicologia social*. Buenos Aires: Ediciones Nueva Vision.

Pontalis, J-B. (1963). "Le petit groupe comme objet," in *Après Freud*. Paris: Gallimard, 1993, pp. 257–73.

Rosenberg, B. (1991). *Masochisme gardien de la vie, masochisme mortifère*. Paris: Presses universitaires de France.

Ruffiot, A. (1984). "Le couple et l'amour. De l'originaire au groupal," in A. Eiguer (ed.), *La thérapie psychanalytique du couple*. Paris: Bordas, pp. 85–145.

Schaeffer, J. (1997). *Le refus du féminin*. Paris: Presses universitaires de France, 2008. English translation: *The Universal Refusal: A Psychoanalytic Exploration of the Feminine Sphere and its Repudiation*. London: Karnac, 2011.

Schaeffer, J. (2002). "Le parcours des antagonismes entre féminin et maternel," in L. Solis-Ponton (ed.), *La parentalité, Défi pour le troisième millénaire*. Paris: Presses universitaires de France, pp. 139–55.

Schaeffer, J. (2007). "D'une possible co-création du masculin et du féminin?" in P. De Neuter and D. Bastien (eds), *Clinique du couple*. Ramonville-Saint-Agne: Erès.

Solis-Ponton, L. (2002). *La parentalité, Défi pour le troisième millénaire*. Paris: Presses universitaires de France.

142 Bibliography

Solis-Ponton, L. (2008). "Le passage du couple conjugal au couple parental: un parcours semé de mines interpersonnelles," in *Dialogue*. Toulouse: Erès.

Smadja, E. (2009). *Le complexe d'Œdipe, cristallisateur du débat psychoanalyse/anthropologie*. Paris: Presses universitaires de France.

Smadja, E. (2013). *Laughter*. London: College Publications. Translation of *Le Rire*. Paris: Presses universitaires de France, 1993, 1996, 2007, 2011.

Willi, Jürg (1975). *Couples in Collusion; the Unconscious Dimension in Partner Relationships*. New York: Jason Aronson, 1977. Translation of *Zweierbeziehung, Das unbewusste Zusammenspiel von Partnern als Kollusion*. Berlin: Rowohlt Verlag, 1975. French translation: *La relation de couple*. Paris: Delachaux & Niestlé, 1982.

Winnicott, D. W. (1952). "Psychoses and childcare," in *Through Pediatrics to Psychoanalysis. Collected Papers*. New York: Brunner-Routledge, 1958, 219–28.

Winnicott, D. W. (1965). *The Maturational Processes and the Facilitating Environment*. London: Hogarth.

Winnicott, D. W. (1971). *Playing and Reality*. Abingdon: Routledge, 2005.

Index

affective ambivalence 43
aging 92–7; characteristics of
  psychic aging 93–7
Albert and Judith case study 61
alliances, unconscious 31–2, 60–1,
  103, 128
aloneness 22; *see also* living alone
alterity/identity conflict 44–5
anal object-relation 53–4, 102–3
anal–sadistic collusion 26
anal sexuality 95
André, J. 58, 104
angry outbursts 125
Anzieu, D. 29–30, 48, 62, 102, 105
Argentina 28
auto-eroticism 85

Balint, M. 17
basic assumptions 23–4
basic fault 17
basic group 23–4
beginning: love life 62–3; phase of
  sexuality 75
Benveniste, E. 1
Bion, W.R. 22–4, 105
bisexuality 21–2; psychic 46–7;
  psychoanalytic therapy 129–30
Bleger, J. 28
bodily-sexual reality 35, 107–8, 111
Bologne, J.-C. 4, 6, 7, 133
boundaries 101–2, 121
Bouvet, M. 52–4, 102
Bozon, M. 9, 57, 74, 75, 76, 108
Braunschweig, D. 77–8, 85

Brusset, B. 11, 12, 14, 17
Burguière, A. 4, 6–7
Bydlowski, M. 80, 92

Caillot, J.-P. 32–3
canon law 4
castration 95; fear of 45
Calvin, J. 5
celibacy 4, 5
childless couple 88–92
children: birth of 81–5; desire for a child
  79–81, 125–7; grandparenthood 96–7;
  parenthood 81–8; presence of
  symptoms in 114
choice: childlessness by free choice 88–90;
  of partner 19, 56–61, 124
Christianity 4–5
Church 6, 7, 8, 133
civil marriage 8
civilizing process 7
clandestine marriages 5
Classical period 6
cohabitation 4, 6, 8, 9; *see also* living
  together
collusion 25–7
communication 22; conjugal 69–71;
  suffering couple 113
complaints 124–5
concern, capacity for 21
conflicts 34, 104–5, 132–3, 136; conflict
  of finitude 93–4; fundamental psychic
  components 44–6; 'natural' history
  72–3; parenthood 87–8; psychoanalytic
  therapy 113–14, 124–7

144 Index

conjugal couples (long-term couples) 27, 28
conjugal crisis *see* crisis
conjugal culture and identity 67–79
conjugal economy 34, 67, 106
conjugal Ego 105–7
conjugal group 101–2, 103–4
conjugal life 67–79; exploration of different areas of 116–18; organization of 68–9, 127
conjugal models, crisis of 137–8
conjugal Self 33, 50–1, 128–9
conjugal socialization work 104
container/contained relationship 24
contemporary society 8–9, 134–7; narcissistic and perverse 135–6; new modes of forming couples 8–9, 133–4; paradoxical trends 134–5
contraception 75
contract, marriage as 5, 6
contra-indications for therapy 118–19
Council of Trent 5, 6
counter-transference 118, 128
couple-object 32–3
couple pathologies 110
couple work 37, 73, 100–12, 130, 136–8; failures of 109–10, 130, 137; functions of 110–11; impact on the partners' psychic organization and functioning 108–9; normality and pathology in couples' lives together 110; within psychic reality 101–5; within sexual-bodily reality 107–8; within socio-cultural reality 105–7
Cournut, J. 45–6
creativity 21
crisis 34, 63–6; post-critical evolving possibilities 66–7; potentially critical stages 64
cross-identifications 21
culture, baby of the 86

Danon-Boileau, H. 93, 94, 95, 96
David, C. 46–7, 58
de Singly, F. 82, 83, 104, 108
Decherf, G. 32–3
defense mechanisms, primitive 19

defensive unconscious alliances 31–2, 60
delusional jealousy 47–8
depressive position 18, 21
desire, sexual 77–8
desire for a child 79–81; conflict about 125–7
destruction instinct 43, 51
Dicks, H.V. 25
differences 72
disenchantment with love 72
divorce 5, 8, 9, 133–4
domestic organization 68–9, 127
dream model 29–30
durability 137–8

Ego 15–16, 93–4, 104–5; conflict with object 54; conjugal 105–7; Freud and analysis of 14–15
Eiguer, A. 33
Elias, N. 7
Enlightenment 6–7
envy 19, 20, 47–8
Eros 43, 51
'erotic chain' 39–40, 76
erotic life *see* sexuality
erotic sexuality 134–5
exogamy, law of 3
exploration of conjugal life 116–18
extra-conjugal acting 64–6, 114
Ezriel, H. 28

Fain, M. 77–8, 85
Fairbairn, W.R.D. 17–18
family 32–3, 134; birth of a child 81–5; grandparenthood 96–7; as institution and the history of marriage 1–2, 4, 5–6, 133; parenthood 81–8
family-object 32
fantasies 48–9; fantasizing in psychoanalytic therapy 121; groups 29–30; suffering couple 128
fantasized baby 86
father role 82–3
Faure-Pragier, S. 79–80, 81, 90–2
female/male conflict 45–6
female sexuality 16, 75–6, 78–9
female sterility 90–2
Ferenczi, S. 17

Index 145

fetishism 16
feudal society 5
floating projections 25
Foulkes, S.H. 28–9
fragility of contemporary couples 9, 133–4
France 6, 8; contemporary conceptions 32–6; group psychoanalysis 29–32
Francescato, D. 72
French language 2; definitions of couple 2–3
Freud, S. 11–16, 43, 51, 79–80; jealousy 15, 47–8
functional sexuality 95
functioning, exploration of 117
fundamental psychic components 39–55; conflicts 44–6; envy and jealousy 47–8; fantasy life 48–9; fusional and symbiotic aspects 50–1; instinctual and affective ambivalence 43; narcissism 40–3; object-relations 51–4; Œdipus and sibling complexes 48; pregenital aspects 43–4; projections and identifications 49–50; psychic bisexuality 46–7; sexuality and the 'erotic chain' 39–40; transference within the couple 51
fusion 50–1

Garcia, V. 111
genital object-relation 52
Germanic peoples 4
Godelier, M. 9, 81–2
'goods and services' 69
grandparenthood 96–7
Great Britain 28–9
Green, A. 39–40, 42–3, 45, 49, 54, 104–5
group illusion 62
group level 36, 101–2, 121, 128–9
group mentality 23
group psychoanalysis 28–32
group psychology 14–15
groupal psychic apparatus model 30–2
groups 22–4; conjugal group 101–2, 103–4
Grunberger, B. 40–1, 50, 53, 102, 120

hate 18, 43
Héran, F. 57
Héritier, F. 3, 74, 79, 88

historical overview 4–8
historical points of reference 11–38; Bion 22–4; contemporary French conceptions 32–6; Dicks 25; Freud 11–16; group psychoanalysis 28–32; Klein 18–20; Lemaire 27–8; object-relation 11–12, 17–18; Willi 25–7; Winnicott 20–2
homosexuality 15; female 9, 15; Freud 15; heterosexuals' extra-conjugal acting with homosexual partners 66; homosexual couples in contemporary society 9
'honeymoon' phase 62–3
hygienic sexuality 135
hypercomplexity 136

Id 15–16, 93–4, 105
identifications 49–50; introjective 20, 21; projective 20, 21, 24
identity: conflict with alterity 44–5; conjugal culture and 67–79
identity models, crisis in 137–9
illusion 21; group illusion 62
imaginary baby 86
inadequacy 113
inconception 91
individualism 133, 134, 137
Indo-European language 1, 2
instincts 13; instinctual ambivalence 43
interfantasizing 33
internal groups 30–1
internal object 18
interpretation 121–2
intersubjective level 36, 122, 129; couple work 102–4
intersubjectivity work 32, 104
inter-transferential neurosis 35, 51
intrapsychic-individual level 36, 104–5, 122, 129
introjective identification 20, 21
investment, parental 84–5

jealousy 15, 19–20, 47–8
Judith and Albert case study 61

Kaës, R. 30–2, 49, 59–60, 101, 104
Kaufmann, J.-C. 8, 57, 68, 69–70, 72
kinship 3
Klein, M. 18–20

146 Index

Latin 1, 2
Le Goués, G. 93–4, 95
Lebovici, S. 86
Lemaire, J.-G. 27–8, 58, 66–7, 73
linguistics 1–3
Littre, E. 2–3
living alone 9, 133–4
living together 4, 6, 8, 9; developing a
    conjugal culture and identity 67–79
long-term couples (conjugal couples) 27, 28
losses, aging and 93, 95–6
Louis and Martine case study 123–30
love: disenchantment with 72; fantasy and
    34; and hate 43; history of marriage and
    5, 6–8; primary 17; risk of intense love 59
love affairs: extra-conjugal acting 64–6,
    114; short-term couples 27
love life: Freud 12–13; Klein 18–19
Luquet, P. 49–50
Luther, M. 5

male/female conflict 45–6
male sexuality 75–6, 78–9
male sterility 92
marriage 1–8, 133; contemporary society
    8–9; historical overview 4–8; linguistics
    1–2; traditional societies 3–4
marriage contracts 5, 6
Martine and Louis case study 123–30
masochism 44, 103; good 137
masturbation 95
medicalization 75, 135
meeting 56–61
meeting places 57
melancholia 14
'mentalized' sexuality 95
Middle Ages 5
Missenard, A. 29
mobility 135
morality 135
Morin, E. 136
mother–infant relationship 20, 22, 24
mother role 82–3
mourning 14, 63–4
mutual requirements 134

narcissism 40–3; Freud 13; respect and
    restoration of patients' 120
narcissistic baby 86

narcissistic collusion 25–6
'natural' history 56–99; aging together
    92–7; birth of a child and parenthood
    81–8; childless couple 88–92; conflicts
    72–3; couple crisis 63–6; desire for a
    child 79–81; 'honeymoon' phase 62–3;
    living together 67–71; meeting and
    choosing a partner 56–61; post-critical
    evolving possibilities 66–7; sexuality
    74–9; structuring of couples 60–1
new modes of couple formation 8–9, 133–4
nineteenth century 7–8
normal jealousy 47–8
normality 110

object: bad objects 59; choice of 58–60;
    Ego/object conflict 54; Freud 11; Klein
    18; small group as 29
object-relations 17–18; anal 53–4, 102–3;
    Freud 11–12; fundamental psychic
    components 51–4; oral 53, 102–3
oceanic feeling 16
œdipal conflict: childless couple 89–90;
    sterility 91
œdipal organization 84–5
Œdipus complex 15–16, 26, 46, 48
offensive unconscious alliances 32
oral collusion 26
oral object-relation 53, 102–3
oral sexuality 95
organ sexuality 95
organization of domestic life 68–9, 127
organizers 101

paradoxical social trends 134–5
Parat, C. 15, 84–5, 102
parental imagos 128
parenthood 81–8; mother and father
    roles 82–3
patient–analyst relationship 22, 24
penis envy 16, 20, 91–2
permanent structure 33
personal territories 68–9
perversions 16
phallic–œdipal collusion 26
phoric functions 31, 32
Pichon-Rivière, E. 28
Pontalis, J.-B. 29
post-critical reactions 66–7

pregenital aspects 43–4
pregenital object-relation 52–4
prenatal sojourn 40
primary love 17
processes 101
procreation: separated from sexuality 75;
    see also children
projected jealousy 47–8
projections 49; floating 25
projective identification 20, 21, 24
Protestants 5
psychic bisexuality 46–7
psychic groupality 30–1
psychic reality 35–6; couple work within
    101–5; exploring levels of 128–9;
    functions of couple work 110–11
psychoanalytic therapy 113–31; case
    study 123–30; characteristics of
    the analytical consultation 114–16;
    circumstances of the first consultation
    113–14; establishment of the framework
    119; exploration of areas of conjugal
    life 116–18; indications and contra-
    indications 118–19; objectives and
    benefits 122–3; preliminary interviews
    114–18; request for 117; technical
    aspects 119–22
psychologization 75, 135

Renaissance 5–6
repairing function 111
representations of a baby 86–7
requirements, mutual 134
retirement 95–6
reverie 24
Rickman, J. 28
Riviere, J. 19
roles: defining 68–9; parental 82–3
Romans, the 4
Rosenberg, B. 43, 44, 103
Ruffiot, A. 33–4, 63
rules for psychoanalytic therapy 119

sadism 44
Schaeffer, J. 78
separations 9, 133–4
sexual-bodily reality 35, 107–8, 111
sexual continuity 9, 134
sexual disorders 77

sexuality 9; aging and 94–5; and the 'erotic
    chain' 39–40, 76; female 16, 75–6,
    78–9; Freud 12, 16; Klein 19–20; male
    75–6, 78–9; 'natural' history 74–9; new
    centrality of 134–5
short-term couples (love affairs) 27
sibling complex 48, 59–60
'sibling' couple 90
socialization 8; conjugal socialization
    work 104
socio-cultural reality 35, 105–7, 111
Solis-Ponton, L. 85, 86, 87
stabilization phase 75
State 6, 7, 133
sterile couple 88, 90–2
structuring of couples 33, 60–1
structuring unconscious
    alliances 31
suffering couple 113–31, 138;
    case study 123–30; *see also*
    psychoanalytic therapy
symbiosis 50–1
symptomatic exploration 116–17

territories, personal 68–9
times of trial 64
topography 34
traditional societies: birth of a
    child 81–2; childlessness 88; desire
    for a child 79; images of marriage,
    married couples and celibacy
    3–4; sexuality 74
transference 117–18, 128; Freud and
    transference-love 13–14; within the
    couple 51
trauma-object 54
twentieth century 8

unconscious alliances 31–2, 60–1,
    103, 128

Vedic 2
verbal communication 71
violence 114

Willi, J. 25–7, 101–2
Winnicott, D.W. 20–2, 50
work couple 68, 69, 105
work group 23, 29